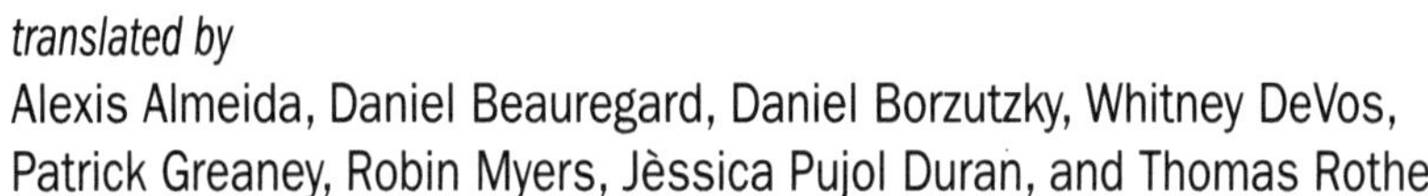

translated by
Alexis Almeida, Daniel Beauregard, Daniel Borzutzky, Whitney DeVos,
Patrick Greaney, Robin Myers, Jèssica Pujol Duran, and Thomas Rothe

Carlos
Soto
Román

Originally published in Spanish as *11* (Santiago, 2017)

ISBN: 978-1-946433-97-8
First Edition, First Printing, 2023
750 copies

Ugly Duckling Presse
The Old American Can Factory
232 Third Street, #E-303
Brooklyn, NY 11215
uglyducklingpresse.org

Design: Joaquín Contreras / Carbón
Cover design: Rebekah Smith
Cover art © Jorge Tacla, *Identidad Oculta 163* (2022).
Oil and marble powder on canvas. 64 x 78 inches / 162.6 x 198.2 cm.

Printed & bound in Saline, MI by McNaughton & Gunn

Distribution: SPD | Small Press Distribution
spdbooks.org

The publication of this book was made possible, in part, by the
New York State Council on the Arts with the support of the Office
of the Governor and the New York State Legislature.

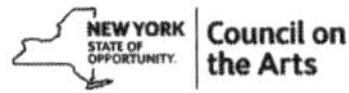

11

Carlos Soto Román

translated by
Alexis Almeida, Daniel Beauregard, Daniel Borzutzky, Whitney DeVos,
Patrick Greaney, Robin Myers, Jèssica Pujol Duran, and Thomas Rothe

Memory is lost
Writing endures

Arabic Proverb

Never again...

Attention	post one	post one	post one	post five
move along	over	...		
...	post one	post one	post one	post five
move along	over	...		

Bearing in mind:

1st — The severe economic, social, and moral crisis currently destroying our country;

the patriotic commitment:

to restore the (broken) national spirit
to restore our (broken) justice system
to restore our (broken) institutions

aware that this is the only way:

to uphold   national tradition
to uphold   the legacy of our Founding Fathers
to uphold   the History of Chile

aware that this is the only way:
to guide the country's   progress and evolution
into the future

V I G O R O U S L Y

THE FIRST ONES

Soldiers took two wounded members from the President's security detail inside La Moneda and led them to the General Hospital. They were **Antonio AGUIRRE VÁSQUEZ***, 29, and* **Osvaldo RAMOS RIVERA***, 22, members of the Socialist Party. In both cases, records place them at the General Hospital prior to their subsequent removal by military personnel. Their whereabouts have been unknown ever since.*

WHERE ARE THEY?

CHILEAN DECLARATION OF INDEPENDENCE

THE SUPREME DIRECTOR OF THE NATION

XXXXXXXXXXXXXXXXXXXXXXXXXXXXXXXXXXXXXXXXXXXXXXXXXXXXXXXXXXXXXXXXXXXXXXXXXXXXXXXXXXX
XXXXXXXXXXXXXXXXXXXXXXXXXXXXXXXXXXXXXXXXXXXXXXXXXXXXXXXXXXXXXXXXXXXXXXXXXXXXXXXXXXX
XXXXXXXXXXXXXXXXXXXXXXXXXXXXXXXXXXXXXXXXXXXXXXXXXXXXXXXXXXXXXXXXXXXXXXXXXXXXXXXXXXX
XXXXXXXXXXXXXXXXXXXXXXXXXXXXXXXXXXXXXXXXXXXXXXXXXXXXXXXXXXXXXXXXXXXXXXXXXXXXXXXXXXX
XXXXXXXXXXXXXXXXXXXXXXXXXXXXXXXXXXXXXXXXXXXXXXXXXXXXXXXXXXXXXXXXXXXXXXXXXXXXXXXXXXX
XXXXXXXXXXXXXXXXXXXXXXXXXXXXXXXXXXXXXXXXXXXXXXXXXXXXXXXXXXXXXXXXXXXXXXXXXXXXXXXXXXX
XXXXXXXXXXXXXXXXXXXXXXXXXXXXXXXXXXXXXXXXXXXXXXXXXXXXXXXXXXXXXXXXXXXXXXXXXXXXXXXXXXX
XXXXXXXXXXXXXXXXXXXXXXXXXXXXXXXXXXXXXXXXXXXXXXXXXXXXXXXXXXXXXXXXXXXXXXXXXXXXXXXXXXX
XXXXXXXXXXXXXXXXXXXXXXXXXXXXXXXXXXXXXXXXXXXXXXXXXXXXXXXXXXXXXXXXXXXXXXXXXXXXXXXXXXX
XXXXXXXXXXXXXXXXXXXXXXXXXXXXXXXXXXXXXXXXXXXXXXXXXXXXXXXXXXXXXXXXXXXXXXXXXXXXXXXXXXX
XXXXXXXXXXXXXXXXXXXXXXXXXXXXXXXXXXXXXXXXXXXXXXXXXXXXXXXXXXXXXXXXXXXXXXXXXXXXXXXXXXX
XXXXXXXXXXXXXXXXXXXXXXXXXXXXXXXXXXXXXXXXXXXXXXXXXXXXXXXXXXXXXXXXXXXXXXXXXXXXXXXXXXX
XXXXXXXXXXXXXXXXXXXXXXXXXXXXXXXXXXXXXXXXXXXXXXXXXXXXXXXXXXXXXXXXXXXXXXXXXXXXXXXXXXX
XXXXXXXXXXXXXXXXXXXXXXXXXXXXXXXXXXXXXXXXXXXXXXXXXXXXXXXXXXXXXXXXXXXXXXXXXXXXXXXXXXX
XXXXXXXXXXXXXXXXXXXXXXXXXXXXXXXXXXXXXXXXXXXXXXXXXXXXXXXXXXXXXXXXXXXXXXXXXXXXXXXXXXX
XXXXXXXXXXXXXXXXXXXXXXXXXXXXXXXXXXXXXXXXXXXXXXXXXXXXXXXXXXXXXXXXXXXXXXXXXXXXXXXXXXX
XXXXXXXXXXXXXXXXXXXXXXXXXXXXXXXXXXXXXXXXXXXXXXXXXXXXXXXXXXXXXXXXXXXXXXXXXXXXXXXXXXX
XXXXXXXXXXXXXXXXXXXXXXXXXXXXXXXXXXXXXXXXXXXXXXXXXXXXXXXXXXXXXXXXXXXXXXXXXXXXXXXXXXX
XXXXXXXXXXXXXXXXXXXXXXXXXXXXXXXXXXXXXXXXXXXXXXXXXXXXXXXXXXXXXXXXXXXXXXXXXXXXXXXXXXX
XXXXXXXXXXXXXXXXXXXXXXXXXXXXXXXXXXXXXXXXXXXXXXXXXXXXXXXXXXXXXXXXXXXXXXXXXXXXXXXXXXX
XXXXXXXXXXXXXXXXXXXXXXXXXXXXXXXXXXXXXXXXXXXXXXXXXXXXXXXXXXXXXXXXXXXXXXXXXXXXXXXXXXX

Bernardo O'Higgins

Miguel Zañartu   *Hipólito de Villegas*   *José Ignacio Zenteno*

The following persons must surrender voluntarily to the Ministry of National Defense by 4:30 p.m., today, September 11, 1973.

Failure to present oneself in person will be considered a rejection of measures taken by the Government Junta Commanders in Chief; offenders will be subject to foreseeable consequences.

<u>C E R T I F I C A T E</u>

I, the undersigned Director of the Office of Detainee Control,

hereby certify that ______________________________ was de-

tained in the National Stadium from _______to _________

____ .⁻

SANTIAGO, _______of_______________ 1973.

Dir. Office of Detainee Control

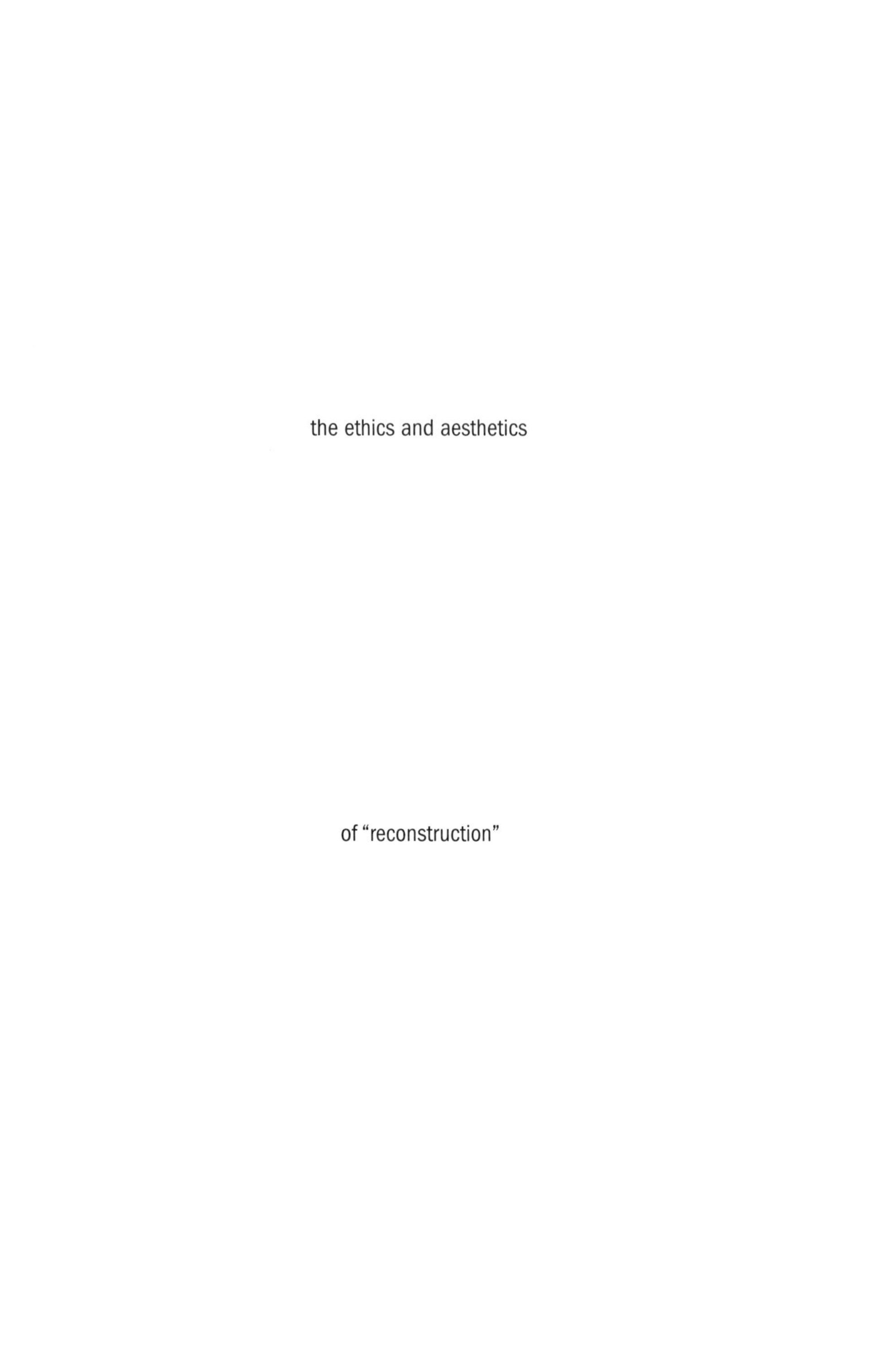

the ethics and aesthetics

of "reconstruction"

*In a noble and chivalrous gesture of military gallantry, the Government Junta's Delegate for the Central Bank of Chile in Valparaíso kisses the hand of one of the many patriotic ladies who congregated in the first-floor offices of the bank this morning to donate jewels, coins, and other valuables, as part of the impromptu citizens' campaign known as the "Fund for National Economic Restoration." The commander holds in his left hand a special receptacle to receive the money and valuables, which will be safeguarded in the bank's vaults.

CHILEAN ARMY
DIVISION V.
COMMAND HEADQUARTERS: AREAS IN STATE OF SIEGE

ORDINANCE #_____

<u>WHEREAS</u>:

1. Banknotes with political propaganda or any other type of illegitimate deed remain in circulation.

2. Our Nation and the prompt restoration of its public order are of the utmost present concern, the immediate dissolution of party politics is required.

<u>DECREE</u>:

Commanding Officer, Areas in State of Siege

TRANSMITTED AT 16:00

<u>DISTRIBUTION</u> :
— In accordance with Plan A.1.

- For having buried a count of 15 weapons, a sizable quantity of ammunition, and explosives
- For having participated in guerrilla warfare training
- For stealing explosives
- For inciting miners to seize armories
- For inciting support of armed resistance
- For having participated in the acquisition and distribution of firearms
- For being caught with buried explosives

Citizens are hereby informed that today, ___ of ___________, _______ at 16:00 hours the following persons were executed pursuant to what was mandated by the Military Tribunals in times of War:

– for violating state security laws

– for belonging to terrorist organizations

– for professing ideologies incompatible with the soul of the nation

I hereby order:

— that he be detained and brought before the authorities
— that he be brought before the relevant security agencies for interrogation in the interest of gathering information toward the prevention of subversive acts
— that he be relegated to the municipality of

to be published and archived,

Ministry of the Interior
Santiago, April ______

the worker l s l z rd

the teacher m rc l g zm n

the fishery inspector n lb rt c ñ s

the conscript m ch l n sh

the navy officer j n c ld r n

the navy officer j n j m n z

the lawyer j l c b z s

the port administrator j s c rd v

the civil servant j n v l nc

the customs official m r m rr s

the schoolteacher h mb rt l z r d

the geographer fr dd t v rn

the municipal employee j s s mps n

the customs officer j n r z

the fishing boat captain r d lf f nz l d

the carpenter g rm n p l m n s

the factory worker m n l s nh z

...in order to expedite processes and standardize criteria in the administration of justice with respect to political prisoners.

.

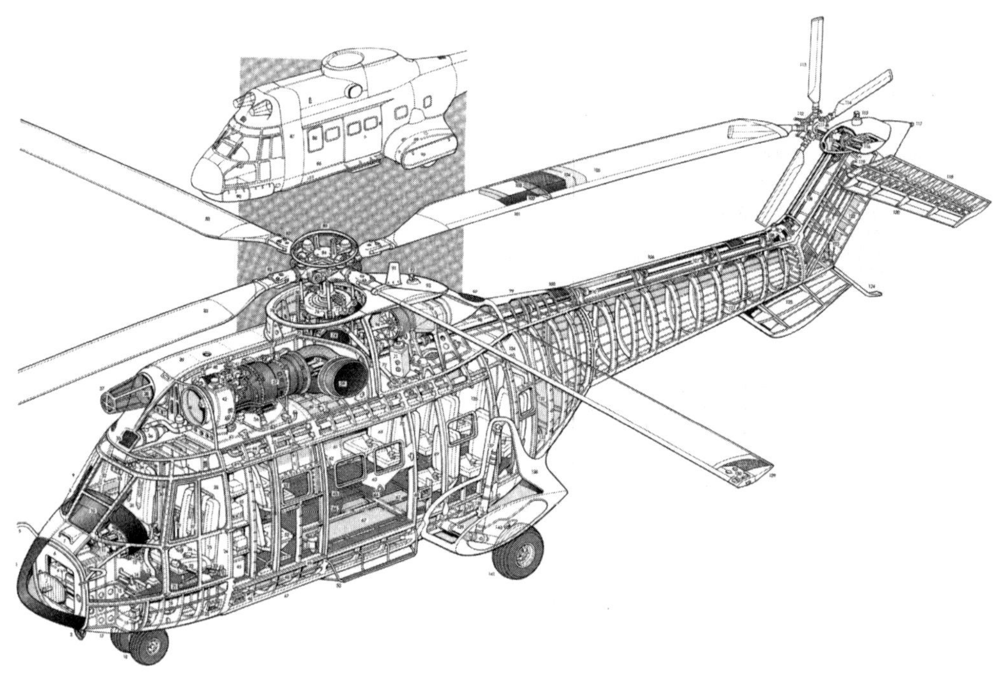

incompetent
pushovers
sissies
cowards

weak commanders

Rancagua
Curicó
Talca
Linares
Concepción
Temuco
Valdivia
Puerto Montt
Cauquenes

La Serena

Copiapó

Antofagasta

Calama

Iquique

Pisagua

Arica

First the legs, then the sexual organs, then the heart.

They fired the machine guns in this order.

CHILEAN ARMY
CAJSI.II.D.E.

3550/ 555

SANTIAGO, OF , 1974

FROM THE COMMANDER IN CHIEF OF AJSI.II.D.E.
TO THE MMES.

   and

      .

I hereby acknowledge receipt of your letter of the of ,
1973, in which you have requested information with regard
to the circumstances of the deaths of your husbands

    ,   ,

and   .

According to the documents on file at the Command
Headquart in my charge, your husbands were executed
after they were caught firing on the Bío Bío Milit. Housing
Complex on the of , 1973.

Consistent with your request, I hereby inform you that an
investigation is currently underway given that your letter
contains the name of a Sergeant who is not affiliated with
any Unit under my command.

Yours sincerely,

Brigadier General
Commander in Chief of the AJSI.II.D.E.

E

N   S

W

GUARDS

reservoir

BARBED WIRE   mountains

SOLDIERS

guard

river

PRISONERS

guard

BARRIER

GUARD

BRIDGE

river

DESERT

desert

At approximately 16:00 hours, in the vicinity of the Arica Regiment, a powerful blast of machine gun fire was heard, occurring without question at the time of the mass murder.

APPLICATION OF THE "ESCAPE LAW"

1. Shot
2. Shot
3. Shot
4. Shot
5. Shot
6. Shot

1ˢᵗ WAR TRIBUNAL

1. Executed
2. Executed
3. Executed
4. Executed
5. Executed

NATIONAL STADIUM SCOREBOARD
NOVEMBER 21, 1973

YOUTH AND SPORT
UNITE CHILE TODAY

FIFA WORLD CUP
1974

CHILE   1
SOVIET U.   0

EXECUTIVE ORDER NO. 521 (1974)

(Published in the Official Journal No. 28,879, June 18, 1974)

NO. 521– Santiago, June 14, 1974

Pursuant to: The stipulations of Executive Orders Nos. 1 and 128 of 1973 and

Whereas the Supreme Governing Body prescribes the immediate and permanent cooperation of a specialized agency that shall consistently provide it with the duly processed information required to adapt its resolutions in the area of Security and National Development.

The Government Junta hereby decrees the following

EXECUTIVE ORDER:

~~ARTICLE 1 There is hereby established the Directorate of National Intelligence, professional technical military agency directly subordinate to the Government Junta, the mission of which shall be to gather all information, on the national level, from the different operational areas, for the purpose of producing the intelligence required to formulate policies and plans, as well as to adopt measures toward securing the protection of national security and development.~~

EXTERMINATED
LIKE RATS

the defense of State security
the defense of public order
the fight against terrorism

CERTIFICATE

=========

I hereby certify that   was detained in the Aerial Warfare Academy, on orders of the undersigned, from   to
of the same month, of   , and was released for lack of sufficient evidence against her.

This CERTIFICATE is hereby granted at the request of her spouse Mr.   , and shall be presented before the Ministry of Defense, without prejudice to any other charges held by said Court.

SANTIAGO,   of   ,   .-

Colonel of Aviation (A)
PROSECUTOR OF AVIATION

CERTIFICATE

THE __COLONEL__, NATIONAL EXECUTIVE SECRETARY
FOR PRISONERS, who signs;

CERTIFIES

That the citizen ___________________,
Identification Card # _________________, Cabinet of ___SANTIAGO___,
remained imprisoned in: __PUNTA ARENAS and DAWSON ISLAND__ . - ======
===
from: _______________________ to _______________________________

That this arrest was a provisional consequence of the application of the powers granted by the State of Siege.

That the prisoner has been released due to insufficient evidence, until this date, of violating the Country's constitutional regulations.

Submitted in Santiago on the _________________day, of the month of _______________________, of the year nineteen seventy-five.

Colonel
National Executive Secretary

C.AS.-

the tribunal confirmed:

A — Violation of the rights of man and of the rights of peoples.

1 — Which, far from having diminished, after the first sentence, the repression has not failed to intensify in _______, in Chile, in _________ and in _______; that the definitive assessment of this first decision, namely, that the governments of these four States are guilty of serious, repeated, and systematic violations of the rights of man, has been confirmed by the supplementary information provided to this Tribunal;

For these reasons
THE TRIBUNAL

On the rights of man

Recalls that in its Rome session it declared the de facto authorities who exercise power in ________, Chile, __________, and __________ to be guilty of serious, repeated, and systematic violations of the rights of man, and confirms this sentence;

Furthermore, taking into account the magnitude of the aforementioned violations, it declares that taken together they constitute a crime against humanity, committed in each of these four countries by the same de facto authorities;

Declares the activities of multinational corporations to be threats to the sovereignty and the rights of peoples;

Declares that the activities of multinational corporations and of other foreign investors in Latin America justify their nationalization, either without compensation, in the form of sanctions, or by reducing their excessive profits;

Declares as well that the payments made to multinational corporations by illegitimate and repressive governments are in violation of the nationalization laws and the rights of peoples, lack all validity, and eliminate all statutes of limitations for those who have received these payments and those who have carried them out.

Denounces the attempts made by multinational corporations to be recognized as plaintiffs by international law; declares that they should be exclusively subject to national jurisdictions and that the establishment of special jurisdictions and agreements between States and multinational corporations is in violation of international law;

Declares that some among them have become coauthors of the fascist coups, as in the case of I.T.T. in Chile;

Condemns those persons and authorities who have appropriated power by force and who exercise it in disregard to the rights of their peoples;

Condemns with these charges the persons who presently exercise power in ______________, Chile, ____________, ______________, ______________, ________, ______________, and ______________;

The Tribunal declares that in the case of the Military Junta led by General Pinochet in Chile, it is found to be in total violation of international law and does not deserve to be considered a member of the organized community of nations.

Condemns the government of the United States, who encouraged these actions; condemns, therefore, President Nixon, who ordered them, and President Ford, who justifies and continues them, and the leaders of the United States, and, more specifically, Mr. Henry Kissinger, whose responsibility in the fascist coup in Chile is in evidence for the Tribunal in the documents published in the United States itself.

THE TRIBUNAL

Demands the immediate release of all persons detained for their political activities and opinions.

Expresses its deep concerns regarding the violations of international law and the rights of the people in _________________; underscores the role of foreign interests in these violations and declares its intention to carry out a complete investigation through all possible and appropriate channels, including the dispatching of an ad hoc committee, with the goal of producing a definitive statement in its third session regarding the situation of this country and the responsibility of its government.

Declares, furthermore, in the case of _______________, that it will proceed to carry out supplementary investigations in the course of its next session.

In the course of this next session, it will also have to determine with the utmost clarity:
-the nature and reach of the military and police interventions of the United States in Latin America;
-the influence of military training acquired by members of Latin American armed forces in the war schools in the United States;
-the role of the multinational corporations in the process of deculturizing the Latin American people;
-the nature of the interdependent ties between political authorities and private economic forces, to determine who bears core responsibility.

THE TRIBUNAL

Agrees that a copy of this decision will be submitted to the national and international authorities included in its verdict.

Brussels, January 1975

RUSSELL TRIBUNAL II

President:

Lelio Basso   Senator of the Italian Independent Left

Vice Presidents:

Vladimir Dedijer   Yugoslav historian
Gabriel García Márquez   Colombian author
François Rigaux   Professor of International Law, Catholic University of Louvain
Albert Soboul   Professor, La Sorbonne

Members:

Juan Bosch   Ex-President of the Dominican Republic
George Casalis   Protestant theologian
Julio Cortázar   Argentine author
Giulio Girardi   Catholic theologian
Uwe Holtz   Member of the Social Democratic Party of Germany and the FRG
                             Nobel Laureate in Physics
Alfred Kastler   Member of the Social Democratic Party of Denmark, union leader
John Molgaard   Professor of Sociology, New York University
James Petras   President of the Commission of Inquiry into United States War
Pham Van Bach   Crimes in Vietnam
                             Mathematician
Laurent Schwartz   National Secretary of the FLM (Italy)
Alberto Tridente   Professor of International Law and ex-ambassador for Chile in
Armando Uribe   Peking

1. Envelope containing checkbooks, account statements, and canceled checks.

2. Various documents related to his status as an employee of

3. Various leaflets.

4. a) Personal effects: 3 pipes, a tobacco pouch, medication.

   b) 82 escudos in bills.

      38.42 escudos in coins.

5. A leather pipe holder shaped like a horseshoe.

6. Nine dictionaries. Five books on various subjects.

7. Several magazines.

8. Three paintings and a photograph.

9. A tray, a cup and saucer, a glass, and a jug.

DATE OF DEATH _________________________________ TIME ____________________

PLACE OF DEATH ____

OBSERVATIONS ____

Cause: Cervical thoracic trauma.

Cause: Cardiopulmonary arrest. Head injury by firearm.

Cause: Destruction of the thorax and cardiac region. Execution.

HABEAS CORPUS

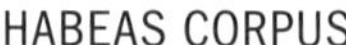

(you shall have the body)

PRIMARY MATTER: Writ of amparo
ANCILLARY PETITION: Review of documents
ADDENDUM PETITION: Proceedings

                              HON. COURT

                , employee, residing at   street
to this hon. court of law:

        I present an appeal for the writ of amparo in favor of

                              THEREFORE
                              I BEG THIS HON. COURT
                              ANCILLARY PETITION: I BEG THIS HON. COURT
                              ADDENDUM PETITION: I BEG THIS HON. COURT

SEPTEMBER 21, 1976 – WASHINGTON DC
THE WHITE HOUSE

7:33 The President had breakfast.

8:02 The President went to the doctor's office.

8:10 The President went to the Oval Office.

9:05 The President met with John O. March Jr., Counselor.

9:20 The President met with Richard B. Cheney, Assistant.

10:15 The President met with his Assistant for National Security Affairs.
10:15 The President met with his Assistant for National Security Affairs.
10:15 The President met with his Assistant for National Security Affairs.
10:15 The President met with his Assistant for National Security Affairs.

SPEECH AT CHACARILLAS

(trumpets)

(torches) (applause) (cheers: Pinochet! Pinochet! Pinochet!)
(torches) (applause) (cheers: Pinochet! Pinochet! Pinochet!)
(torches) (applause) (cheers: Pinochet! Pinochet! Pinochet!)
(torches) (applause) (cheers: Pinochet! Pinochet! Pinochet!)
(torches) (applause) (cheers: Pinochet! Pinochet! Pinochet!)
(torches) (applause) (cheers: Pinochet! Pinochet! Pinochet!)
(torches) (applause) (cheers: Pinochet! Pinochet! Pinochet!)
(torches) (applause) (cheers: Pinochet! Pinochet! Pinochet!)
(torches) (applause) (cheers: Pinochet! Pinochet! Pinochet!)
(torches) (applause) (cheers: Pinochet! Pinochet! Pinochet!)
(torches) (applause) (cheers: Pinochet! Pinochet! Pinochet!)
(torches) (applause) (cheers: Pinochet! Pinochet! Pinochet!)

(trumpets)

My dear young people:

The future of Chile is always in you, whose glory we are now sculpting.

Chile is you

Homeland, flag, and youth

military star (10 years of service)
star of military merit (20 years of service)
grand star of military merit (30 years of service)
star of minerva (regular course of the war academy)
medal of the goddess minerva (professor of the war academy)
decoration by the president of the republic
first class insignia - medal of valor

11/25 pinochet's birthday. the military band plays "happy birthday"

11/25 pinochet's birthday. the military band plays "the old banners"

11/25 pinochet's birthday. the military band plays "the radetzky march"

11/25 pinochet's birthday. the military band plays "free"

11/25 pinochet's birthday. the military band plays "lili marleen"

thank you

Mr. President, for everything you've done for Chile
for our safety
for our children

God bless you

1810 **CHILE** 1973

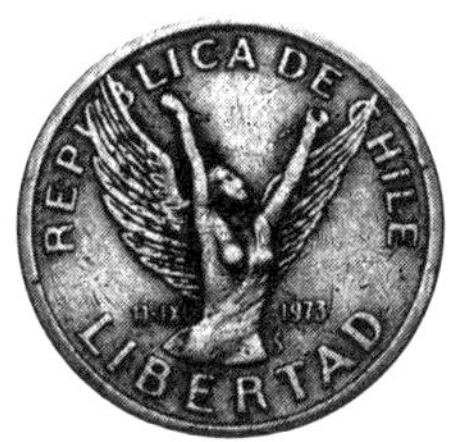

message from the SUPREME GOVERNMENT to those who

the SUPREME GOVERNMENT is working quickly to

spreading subversive propaganda against the SUPREME GOVERNMENT

and threats against the SUPREME GOVERNMENT will be punished

considering that the SUPREME GOVERNMENT needs

the SUPREME GOVERNMENT to the nation's workers

regarding the measures that the SUPREME GOVERNMENT has adopted

the SUPREME GOVERNMENT analyzed in detail

the SUPREME GOVERNMENT has the firm conviction

the SUPREME GOVERNMENT has stipulated

NATIONAL PLEBISCITE

NEW POLITICAL CONSTITUTION
OF THE REPUBLIC OF CHILE
1980

★   YES   ___

○   NO   ___

H

No. 516432

Santiago, October 21, 1980.-

The following has been decreed today:

No. 1,150.– Whereas, provision of decree
laws No. 1 and 128 of 1973, 527 of 1974, 3464 and 3465
of 1980, and

Considering:

That the Hon. Government Junta

That, to this end, the Hon. Government Junta

That the national sovereign will, expressed, by majority, in a free,
secret, and informed act,

That the National Scrutinizing College has referred

By virtue of these records and invoking the
name of God Almighty

I hereby decree:

Let the Political Constitution of the Republic of Chile be hereby approved,
the official text of which is as follows:

POLITICAL CONSTITUTION OF THE REPUBLIC OF CHILE

CHAPTER I

Foundations of Institutionality

Article 1 .- Men are born free or equal in dignity and rights

The aforementioned should not surprise anyone given the basic pillar of the Government's development strategy is the economic policy implemented as of September 11, 1973. Today this has once again been reaffirmed:

Prices shall be freely determined

Deficits in public finances shall not be tolerated

The capital market with free interest rates shall be the mechanism

Interest groups shall not be favored

The role of the State shall be progressively reduced

Of all the official tasks designated to the undersigned, following direct orders from His Excellency, President of the Republic, the most crucial is the sale of State companies. Among these, national and international bidding shall begin with:

- Pacific Steel Company (CAP)
- Chilean Telephone Company (CTC)
- Chilean Electricity Company (CHILECTRA)
- Interoceanic Navigation Company
- Chile Laboratories Inc.
- Telex Chile S.A.
- Continental Bank
- Chile Oil Co. Holding

Likewise, State-owned companies shall ration their cost structure, especially in remunerations, in order to boost profits, which have deteriorated in recent months.

the dead man _________ comes to me every nite, and i didnt wanna kill him and i didnt even no who he was, i just wanted to make some cash rob a couple cab drivers and come back but he put up a fite and wen i shot him in the head and he didnt die, i took out my nife and jammed it in his neck, and twisted it, but i didnt no wat i was doin and that he was him. i grabbed his cash his documents, the taximeter, and wen i realized who he was i tossed it all but kept the flashlite cause we cant always pay the electric at home, and the money, nuthin but a few pesos, haunts me day and nite and i dont wanna keep livin. forgive me mamita and take care a my babies.

If you wish to verify cases of torture in Chile, you will not find any...

- What is the purpose of the interrogation?
- Has an interrogation plan been prepared?
- Is an appropriate setting for interrogation available?
- Will the interrogation sessions be recorded?
- Is the equipment available?
- Installed?
- Have arrangements been made to feed, bed, and guard the subject as necessary?
- Does the interrogation plan call for more than one interrogator?
- If so, have roles been assigned and schedules prepared?
- Is the interrogational environment fully subject to the interrogator's manipulation and control?
- What disposition is planned for the interrogatee after the questioning ends?
- Is it possible, early in the questioning, to determine the subject's personal response to the interrogator or interrogators?
- What is the interrogator's reaction to the subject? Is there an emotional reaction strong enough to distort results? If so, can the interrogator be replaced?
- If the source is resistant, will noncoercive or coercive techniques be used? What is the reason for the choice?
- Has the subject been interrogated before?
- Is he sophisticated about interrogation techniques?

The Grill

Telegrams

The Dry Submarine

The Wet Submarine

Bucking

The Rack

The Parrot

The Rat

The Telephone

Target Practice

The Parrot's Perch

The Cattle Prod

The Generator

1. Shock Areas: Temples
2.   Neck
3   Armpit
4.   Stomach and abdomen
5   Nipple
6.   Penis
7.   Anus
8.   Thighs
9.   Feet
10. Stretcher
11. Electrodes
12. Dynamo or transformer
13. Table
14. Binds

1. Shock Areas: Temples
2.   Neck
3.   Nipple
4.   Penis
5.   Anus
6.   Thighs
7.   Feet
8. Foam mattress
9. Metal bed frame
10. Dynamo and transformer
11. Electrodes
12. Binds tied to cot
13. Table

1. Shock Areas: Feet
2.   Penis
3.   Nipple
4.   Neck
5.   Armpit
6. Water
7. Bathtub
8. Electrodes
9. Dynamo or transformer

they strip me naked and tie me to the __________.
they tie a strap around my head and throw water on my __________.
below the strap, near my temples, they attach some __________.
and on my stomach they put another __________.
they give me electric shocks.
they interrogate me about __________.
they tell me to lift a finger to stop the __________.
this session lasts about __________.

in those first hours I'm examined by a __________.
after that exam, they begin another __________.
this time they check other parts of ________.
and suddenly they stop.
they cover me with a ___________.
and haul me over to the ________.
I hear someone say: "a government minister is coming."

after each session, they took me to ___________.
the doctor, meanwhile, examined me and gave me __________.
one of the strange methods was ___________.
and at the same time they ___________.
I realize I'm in an underground room.
when they strapped me to the ___________.
my body twisted and I _______.
they force me to swallow some __________.
eventually I faint or maybe just pass out.

they changed my blindfold for a __________.
and then quickly put me in a __________.
they told me
they were going to kill me in a __________.
they told me
they were going to dump me in the ocean.

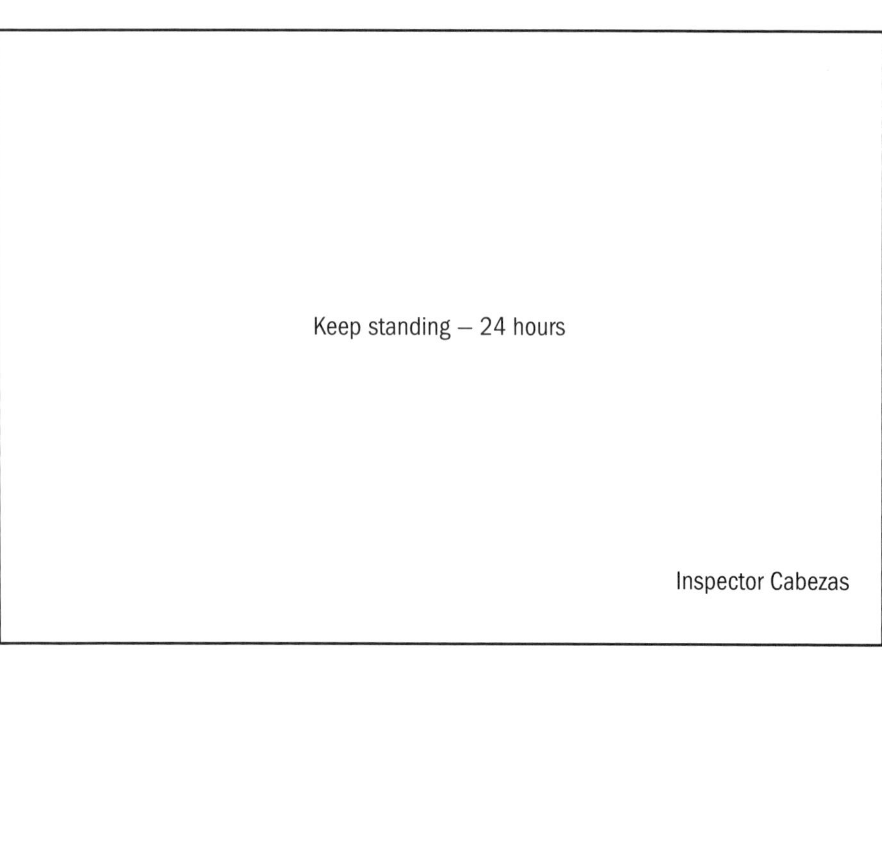

Keep standing — 24 hours
Inspector Cabezas

he was blindfolded for such a long time that he started to develop his sense of hearing, better than us, his sense of smell...

sometimes it was us who would break down at his side when we saw what they were doing to him...

I was punched and kicked, pistol-whipped...

They gave me electric shocks...

Two men brutally raped me...

I was submitted to torture. I was raped...

They hit my ears and gave me electric shocks.

They hit me in the groin, they hit my legs with wet sacks...

I was tied to a post and doused with buckets of water...

They simulated firing squad executions and rapes...

They tore the nails off my pinky toes...

They made me listen to a tape recording of children crying

and told me they were my kids...

I was a month and a half pregnant.
I was two months pregnant.
I was three months pregnant.
I was five months pregnant.
I was six months pregnant.

AGA

CC

CNI

DICAR

DICOMCAR

DIFA

DINA

DINE

SIFA

SIN

SICAR

SIM

"El Mamo"
"The Turd"
"Don Rodrigo"
"Don Elías"
"Luis Gutiérrez"
"Crazy Horse"
"The Cob"
"Raspy"
"The Bear"
"Víctor"
"Antolín"
"Max Lenoux"
"The Wolf"
"Lieutenant Pablo"
"Fatsos"
"The Devil's Doll"
"The Teaspoon"
"The Cat"
"Joel"
"The Beard"
"Bad Motherfucker"
"El Quico"
"Daniel Cáceres"

"Raúl"
"Claudio"
"Don Jaime"
"Lieutenant Manuel"
"Troglodyte"
"Black Hand"
"Dirty Harry"
"Pedro"
"Big Cheeks"
"Small Cheeks"
"The Owl"
"Inspector Cabezas"
"Lalo"
"Fanta"
"El Fifo"
"El Huaso"
"White Fang"
"Wally"
"Willy"
"The Clown"
"Captain Miguel"
"Little Elephant"
"Zambra"

"Peter"
"Crazy Alex"
"The Runt"
"Blondie"
"Pol"
"Rodrigo"
"Small Wally"
"Yerko"
"Jonathan"
"The Chinaman"
"La Comandante"
"Carola"
"Soledad"
"La Negra"
"Pepa"
"Charla"
"Marisol"
"Lint"
"Commander Pepe"
"Ely"
"Carmen Gutiérrez"
"Roxana"
"Pochi"

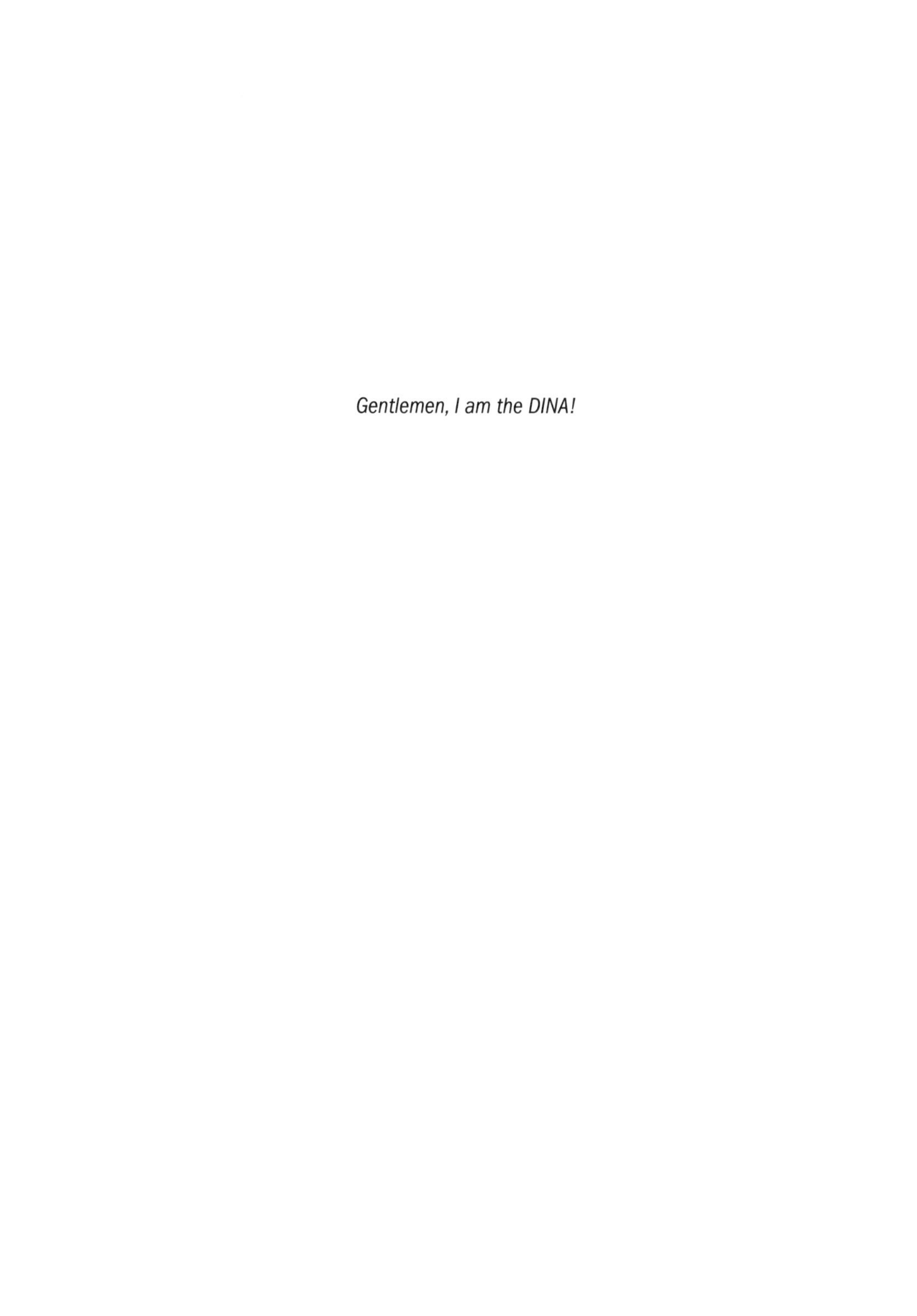
Gentlemen, I am the DINA!

everything seen heard everything in silence forever until the grave

everything seen heard everything in silence forever until the grave

everything seen heard everything in silence forever until the grave

everything seen heard everything in silence forever until the grave

everything seen heard everything in silence forever until the grave

everything seen heard everything in silence forever until the grave

everything seen heard everything in silence forever until the grave

everything seen heard everything in silence forever until the grave

everything seen heard everything in silence forever until the grave

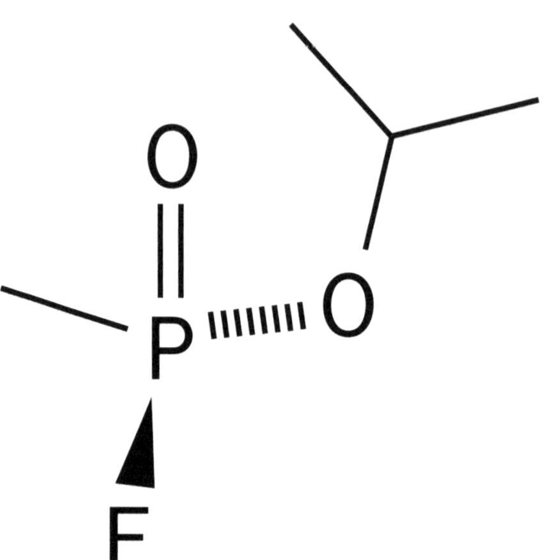

Name IUPAC	(RS)-Propan-2-il metilfosfonofluoridato
General	(RS)-O-Isopropyl methylphosphonofluoridate;
	IMPF;
	GB;
	2-(Fluoro-methylphosphoryl) oxypropane;
	Phosphonofluoridic acid;
	P-methyl-, 1-methylethyl ester

CAS	107—44-82
ChemSpider	7583
PubChem	7871
UNII	B4XG72QGFM

Properties

| Appearance | Clear colorless liquid, brownish if impure |
| | Odorless in pure form |

Density	1.0887 g/cm^3 (25°C)
	1.0887 (25°C)
	1.102 g/cm^3 (20°C)

| Molar Mass | 140.094 g/mol |

| Melting Point | -56°C (217K) |

| Boiling Point | 158°C (431K) |

| Solubility in Water | Miscible |

| Health Hazards | Highly Toxic |

...is a chiral molecule because it has four chemically distinct substituents attached to the tetrahedral phosphorus center. The SP form (the (–) optical isomer) is the more active enantiomer due to its greater binding affinity to acetylcholinesterase. It is manufactured using methylphosphonyl difluoride mixed with isopropyl alcohol.

$$CH_3P(O)F_2 + (CH_3)_2CHOH \rightarrow [(CH_3)_2CHO]CH_3P(O)F + HF$$

Isopropylamine is added to neutralize the hydrogen fluoride generated during this alcoholysis reaction. As a binary chemical weapon, it can be generated in situ by this reaction.

Specifically, it is a potent inhibitor of acetylcholinesterase. It acts on acetylcholinesterase by forming a covalent bond with the particular serine residue at the active site. Fluoride is the leaving group, and the resulting phosphoester is robust and biologically inactive. A buildup of acetylcholine in the synaptic cleft, due to the inhibition of acetylcholinesterase, means the neurotransmitter continues to act on the muscle fiber, so that any nerve impulses are effectively continually transmitted. Normally, acetylcholine is released from the neuron to stimulate the muscle, after which it is degraded by acetylcholinesterase, allowing the muscle to relax. Death will usually occur as a result of asphyxia due to the inability to control the muscles involved in breathing.

...it had the typical smell of a cemetery. You could tell they had been there before to carry out other operations.

Afterward they started throwing them into the ocean, near San Antonio, I think.

Did they do anything to them before throwing them in?

They say they opened them.

Opened them?

Their stomachs. To keep them from floating.

First of all, the fish need to be fed...

No, dumbass, they're prisoners! They're wearing uniforms because they don't have other clothes.

volcano	ocean	ocean	desert
desert	volcano	ocean	ocean
ocean	desert	volcano	ocean
volcano	ocean	desert	volcano
desert	volcano	ocean	desert
ocean	desert	volcano	ocean
volcano	ocean	desert	volcano
volcano	volcano	ocean	desert
ocean	volcano	volcano	ocean
ocean	ocean	volcano	volcano
ocean	ocean	ocean	volcano
desert	ocean	ocean	ocean
desert	desert	ocean	ocean
volcano	desert	desert	ocean
desert	volcano	desert	desert
volcano	desert	volcano	desert
ocean	volcano	desert	volcano
desert	ocean	volcano	desert
ocean	desert	ocean	volcano
volcano	ocean	desert	ocean
volcano	volcano	ocean	desert
desert	volcano	volcano	ocean
ocean	desert	volcano	volcano
desert	ocean	desert	volcano
desert	desert	ocean	desert
ocean	desert	desert	ocean

Military Identification Card

(MIC)

No. 66,650

Expiration Date: 03 Sept 1986

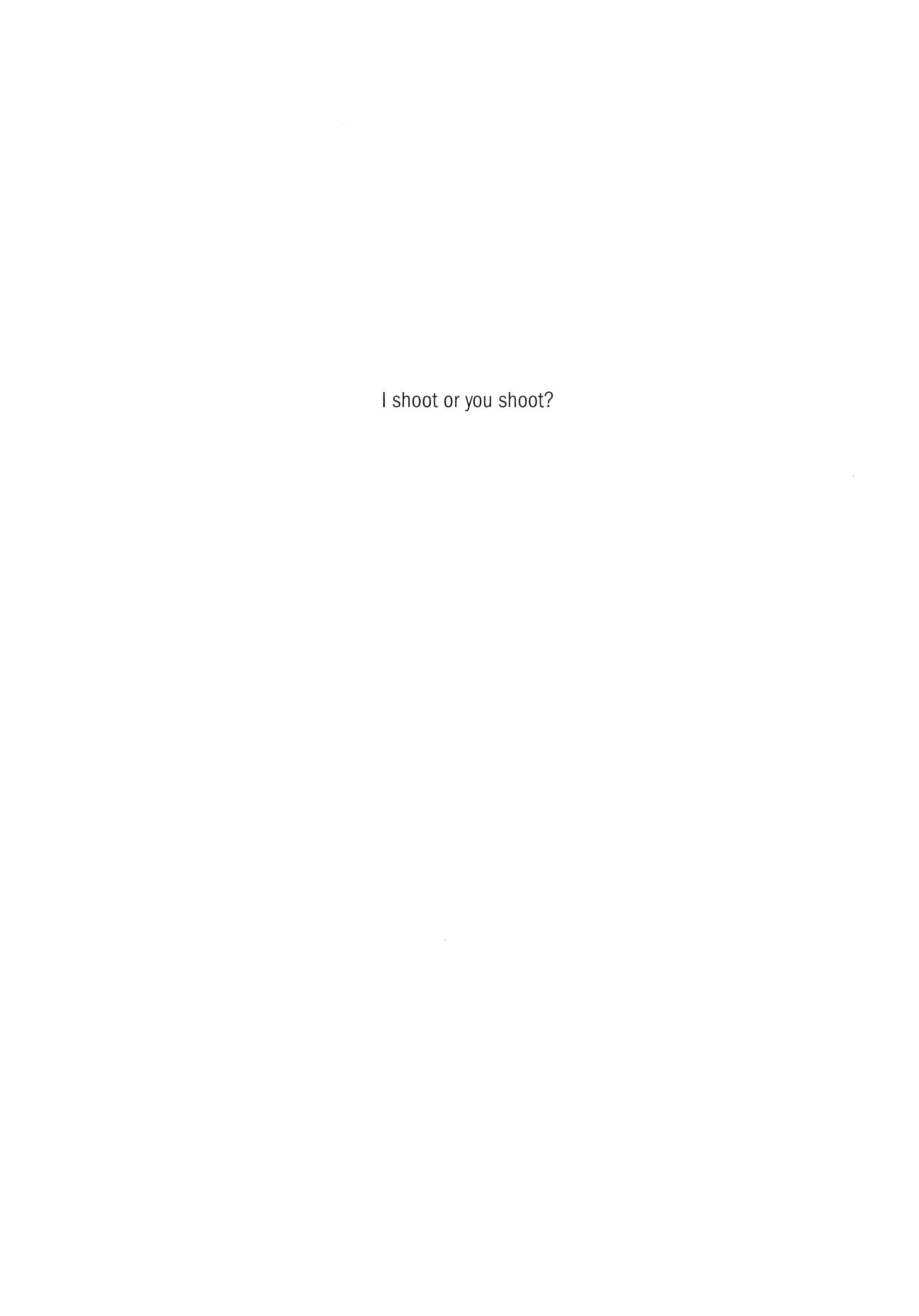
I shoot or you shoot?

(sound of a telegraph)

IT'S THE NEWS HOUR ON RADIO CHILENA

...news of three bodies found just west of Santiago is stirring up drama as the identity of those murdered has yet to be reliably determined.

it is our hope—a church official stated—that there will soon be a truthful and conclusive report, since this is about human life, and we share in the suffering of the families seeking information.

(sound of drums)

RADIO COOPERATIVA KNOWS WHAT'S HAPPENING

...at the same time, a supervisor from the National Coroner's Office has indicated that the government would make an official statement regarding the discovery of the bodies.

we must repeat that family members of people who have been disappeared or kidnapped have congregated outside, making for a dramatic scene upon the vehicle's arrival. This is all the information we have at this moment, live from the Coroner's Office, reported the Daily Cooperativa.

Form #:

Medical Record #:

DRESS AND DELIVER THE CADAVER

of: ____

Santiago, __________ of __________, 19 ___

DATE AND SEAL

Legal Medical Services
Department of Cadaver Reception

How much longer?
How much longer?
How much longer?
How much longer?

Was arrested

on October 26, 1973
on April 30, 1974
on March 27, 1975
on September 15, 1973
on September 28, 1973
on September 12, 1973
on July 8, 1974
on September 15, 1973
on October 9, 1973
on September 16, 1973
on February 14, 1975
on October 4, 1973
on October 16, 1973
on October 16, 1973
on September 7, 1974
on October 6, 1973
on October 11, 1973
on September 18, 1973
on October 8, 1973
on September 14, 1973
on September 27, 1973
on August 23, 1974
on October 17, 1973
on September 20, 1973
on September 4, 1984
on October 4, 1973
on September 11, 1973
on November 6, 1973
on September 11, 1977
on October 10, 1973
on July 30, 1974
on September 16, 1973
on October 6, 1976
on October 7, 1973
on October 7, 1973
on October 6, 1973
on September 15, 1973
on September 15, 1973
on September 17, 1973
on September 12, 1973

by police officers
by police officers
by police officers and members of the army
by police officers
by army troops
by civilian personnel
by police officers
by army troops
by police officers
by members of the National Intelligence Directorate
by police officers and soldiers
by army troops, police officers, and armed civilians from the area
by members of the National Intelligence Directorate
by the police
by police officers
by the police
by the police
by soldiers and police officers
by intelligence agents
by a patrol made up of four police officers
by police officers and armed civilians
by police officers
by detectives
by army troops
by military troops
by soldiers
by uniformed and civilian personnel
by members of the Central Intelligence Directorate
by soldiers
by a patrol of thirty soldiers, police officers, and civilians
by a patrol of thirty soldiers, police officers, and civilians
by a patrol of thirty soldiers, police officers, and civilians
by a patrol of thirty soldiers, police officers, and civilians
by a patrol of thirty soldiers, police officers, and civilians
by a patrol of thirty soldiers, police officers, and civilians
by police officers and civilians
by police officers and civilian collaborators
by police officers and soldiers
by police officers
by members of the Central Intelligence Directorate

on the street

in Población La Victoria

in his home

in San Felipe

in his home

in his home in San Rosendo

in the town of Chabranco

in her home

in his home in downtown Santiago

in his home

in the Campo Lindo settlements

in Tower 12 of the San Borja apartment complex

in her home in Santiago

in his home in Cunco

on the street

in her workplace

on the outskirts of Pucón

in his home in Villa Los Canelos

in his workplace

on Aguas Frescas street in the municipality of Lo Prado

in the La Moneda Palace

in the house of a relative

in Liquiñe

in his home in Santiago

in Chillán

in his home on the El Carmen y Maitenes Estate

in his home in Pemehue Estate

in his home in Fundo El Carmen y Maitenes

in his home in Fundo El Carmen y Maitenes

in his home in Fundo El Carmen y Maitenes

in her parents' house

at his job

at the management office of the Elecmetal company

in his workplace

in his house

in his home in Santiago

in her home in Quinta Normal

in his mother's home

in his home located in the Manso de Velasco neighborhood

in his workplace

Arauco Fisheries

Sudamericana de Vapores Shipping

Federico Santa María Technical University

FELCO

Osorno Spanish Stadium

Valaparaíso Port

ENAMI

Viña Textile Company

Dairy Union of Aconcagua Elecmetal

Catholic University of Valparaíso

Pisagua Prison House Plot 35 Azapa Valley Tarapacá Police Station Building Avenida Santa María Arica Industrial Zone Chacabuco Prison Camp House 2192 Latorre Antofagasta Calama Police Station House 2001 Calle Colo Colo Building Avenida El Estadio La Serena El Belloto Naval Air Base Esmeralda Training Ship Lebu Ship Maipo Ship San Felipe Jail San Antonio Prison House 980 Agua Santa Viña del Mar House 476 Calle Habana Viña del Mar Silva Palma Barracks Valparaíso Investigations San Felipe Police Barracks Isla Riesco Detention Camp Maipo Regiment Valparaíso Melinka-Puchuncaví Prison Camp Premise Industrial Sector Melón Cement La Calera Infantry Regiment No. 3 San Felipe Tejas Verdes Third Precinct of Limache Ritoque Camp San Fernando City Jail Cauquenes Jail Talca Jail Building 262 Ignacio Carrera Pinto Parral Colonia Dignidad Investigations Police Barracks of Cauquenes "El Buen Pastor" Women's Jail Talca Culenar Estate Talca Building 1403 Calle Dos Sur Talca Building Road to Los Niches Curicó Talcahuano Naval Base Casa Grande Concepción Chillán Prison Concepción Prison Los Ángeles Prison Quirihue Prison House on "El Morro" Estate Mulchén "El Buen Pastor" Women's Jail Los Ángeles "Pemehue" Country Estate Mulchén "El Carmen" Country Estate Mulchén House 170 Pedro de Valdivia Concepción Coihueco Police Station Niblinto Police Station San Carlos Police Station Santa Juana Police Station Fourth Precinct of Concepción Police Barracks of Los Ángeles Investigations Police Barracks of Chillán Concepción Regional Stadium El Morro Stadium Talcahuano Fort Borgoño IANSA Gym Building across from Playa Blanca Quiriquina Island German High School Los Ángeles High School for Boys Bulnes Penitentiary San Carlos Prison Yungay Prison Mountain Infantry Regiment No. 17 Los Ángeles Mountain Infantry Regiment No. 9 Chillán Police Checkpoint Avenida España Police Checkpoint Antuco Police Checkpoint in the Zañartu Slum Police Checkpoint Lo Rojas Police Checkpoint Schwager Police Checkpoint San Nicolás Police Checkpoint Santa Bárbara Second Precinct of Chillán Ñuble Highway Police Lieutenancy Coihueco Police Outpost Laja Police Outpost San Rosendo Police Outpost Seventh Precinct of Coronel Temuco Jail Tucapel Regiment Temuco Second Precinct of Temuco Cunco Police Outpost Manquehue Aerial Base Temuco House 764 Calle Pérez Rosales Valdivia Chihuío Country Estate Valdivia House with no address on Calle Magallanes Castro Chiloé Las Bandurrias Bulnes Regiment Third Precinct of Rahue Quellón Police Station Investigations Police Barracks of Puerto Montt House intersection of Obispo Michelatto and Carrera Coyhaique Punta Arenas Old Naval Hospital Catalina Bay Armored Battalion No. 5 Dragon Regiment No. 6 Punta Arenas House 920 Calle Kusma Siuavic Punta Arenas Marine Infantry Detachment No. 4 Fiscal Stadium of Punta Arenas Dawson Island Prison Camp Motorized

Infantry Regiment No. 10 Punta Arenas War Academy Peldehue Special Forces Base Investigations Police Homicide Brigade House on Calle Loyola between Martí and Neptuno House on Apoquindo between Avenida Tobalaba and Apoquindo House at 1453 Avenida Santa María London Clinic Calle Almirante Barroso Santa Lucía Clinic 160 Calle Santa Lucía Maipú Police Station Eighth Precinct of the Investigations Police "Las Tranqueras" Precinct Fourth Precinct Barracks at 1470 Calle Borgoño Barracks at 11 Calle Belgrado Barracks at 1700 Calle Venecia Tres and Cuatro Álamos Prison Camps 3000 Calle Canada National Stadium Military Hospital Implacate Building in the Bellavista Neighborhood Building on Calle Isidora Goyenechea El Bosque Clinic Barros Arana National Boarding School Barracks at 1305 Calle José Domingo Cañas "La Firma" Barracks at 229 Calle Dieciocho Gold pawn shops at 312 Ahumada sixth floor 1061 Moneda 121 Bandera Barracks at 38 Calle Londres Barracks at 245 Calle Maruri Nido 18 Barracks at 9053 Avenida Perú Nido 20 Barracks Cerrillos Airport Hangar Tacna Regiment Remo Cero Barracks Anti-Aircraft Artillery Regiment Colina Compound at Calle Rancagua and José Manuel Infante Compound at 6 Calle Juan Antonio Ríos San Bernardo Infantry Regiment Barrack at 517 Avenida República Maipú Rinconada Barracks Villa Grimaldi Barracks at 8200 Calle José Arrieta Santiago Velodrome "The Sexy Blindfold" Barracks 3037 Calle Irán

<u>PERSONAL FILE</u>

\#

Full Name:

I.D.   Office   Nationality

Address

Occupation

Spouse

Children

Declared Political Affiliation

Circumstances of Arrest
(place, date, time)

RULING

. . . .
SIGNATURE

Was executed

on October 27, 1973
on June 15, 1987
on October 13, 1973
on August 13, 1979
on October 17, 1973
on August 23, 1984
on October 16, 1973
on September 15, 1973
on October 17, 1973
on October 6, 1973
on November 9, 1973
on October 19, 1973
on October 16, 1973
on October 10, 1973
on September 21, 1973
on October 11, 1973
on October 2, 1973
on September 21, 1973
on March 24, 1976
on December 19, 1973
on September 22, 1973
on October 17, 1973
on September 26, 1973
on September 22, 1973
on October 11, 1973
on October 6, 1973
on October 13, 1973
on October 16, 1973
on September 23, 1973
on October 2, 1973
on October 18, 1973
on October 19, 1973
on October 2, 1973
on November 27, 1973
on October 19, 1973
on October 18, 1973
on October 19, 1973
on January 18, 1981
on January 18, 1974
on October 19, 1973

by agents of the State

by personnel of the Yungay 3rd Infantry Regiment

by agents of the National Information Center

by agents of the State

by agents of the National Information Center

by agents of the State

by agents of the National Information Center

by agents of the State

by agents of the State

by agents of the State

by agents of the State

by agents of the State

by agents of the State

by his abductors

by his abductors

by his abductors

by his abductors

by his abductors

by his abductors

by agents of the State

by agents of the State

by agents of the State

by his abductors

by military personnel of the Yungay 3rd Infantry Regiment

by his captors

by Government employees

by his abductors

by his abductors

by his captors

by agents of the Government

by his captors

by his abductors

by military personnel of the Yungay 3rd Infantry Regiment

by agents of the Government

by his captors

by agents of the Government

by agents of the Government

by military personnel

by agents of the Government

by agents of the National Information Center

in the aforementioned building
next to the prison
on Varas Mena Street
on the grounds of the Antofagasta Regional Prison
at the San Juan estate
near the Chihuío Baths
in his house
in the vicinity of her house
in the presence of his family
around La Veleidosa Mine
on the Villarica Bridge over the Toltén River
on the bridge over the Renaico River
on the Bulnes Bridge over the Mapocho River
on the police station patio
in Pelarco
at the San Juan estate
around La Veleidosa Mine
on the road between Calama and Antofagasta
on the road to El Arrayán
on the Pichoy Bridge
on the Pichoy Bridge
inside the mentioned building
at the 26th kilometer on the road to Aysén
on the street
in the Caupolicán Regiment
where he was camping
on the road to Niebla
on the San Juan estate
on the road to Lo Errázuriz
on the road between Calama and Antofagasta
in his home
on the Villarica Bridge over the Toltén River
near her home
on Cardones Hill
on the road between Calama and Antofagasta
on the road between this city and the Cerro Moreno Air Base
in Paso Hondo
in the town of Remeco Alto
in the Caupolicán Infantry Regiment
on the patio of the Aysén Police Precinct

N. N.　N. N.　N. N.　N. N.　N. N.　N. N.　N. N.　N. N.　N. N.　N. N.
N. N.　N. N.　N. N.　N. N.　N. N.　N. N.　N. N.　N. N.　N. N.　N. N.
N. N.　N. N.　N. N.　N. N.　N. N.　N. N.　N. N.　N. N.　N. N.　N. N.
N. N.　N. N.　N. N.　N. N.　N. N.　N. N.　N. N.　N. N.　N. N.　N. N.
N. N.　N. N.　N. N.　N. N.　N. N.　N. N.　N. N.　N. N.　N. N.　N. N.
N. N.　N. N.　N. N.　N. N.　N. N.　N. N.　N. N.　N. N.　N. N.　N. N.
N. N.　N. N.　N. N.　N. N.　N. N.　N. N.　N. N.　N. N.　N. N.　N. N.
N. N.　N. N.　N. N.　N. N.　N. N.　N. N.　N. N.　N. N.　N. N.　N. N.
N. N.　N. N.　N. N.　N. N.　N. N.　N. N.　N. N.　N. N.　N. N.　N. N.
N. N.　N. N.　N. N.　N. N.　N. N.　N. N.　N. N.　N. N.　N. N.　N. N.
N. N.　N. N.　N. N.　N. N.　N. N.　N. N.　N. N.　N. N.　N. N.　N. N.
N. N.　N. N.　N. N.　N. N.　N. N.　N. N.　N. N.　N. N.　N. N.　N. N.
N. N.　N. N.　N. N.　N. N.　N. N.　N. N.　N. N.　N. N.　N. N.　N. N.
N. N.　N. N.　N. N.　N. N.　N. N.　N. N.　N. N.　N. N.　N. N.　N. N.
N. N.　N. N.　N. N.　N. N.　N. N.　N. N.　N. N.　N. N.　N. N.　N. N.
N. N.　N. N.　N. N.　N. N.　N. N.　N. N.　N. N.　N. N.　N. N.　N. N.
N. N.　N. N.　N. N.　N. N.　N. N.　N. N.　N. N.　N. N.　N. N.　N. N.
N. N.　N. N.　N. N.　N. N.　N. N.　N. N.　N. N.　N. N.　N. N.　N. N.
N. N.　N. N.　N. N.　N. N.　N. N.　N. N.　N. N.　N. N.　N. N.　N. N.
N. N.　N. N.　N. N.　N. N.　N. N.　N. N.　N. N.　N. N.　N. N.　N. N.
N. N.　N. N.　N. N.　N. N.　N. N.　N. N.　N. N.　N. N.　N. N.　N. N.
N. N.　N. N.　N. N.　N. N.　N. N.　N. N.　N. N.　N. N.　N. N.　N. N.
N. N.　N. N.　N. N.　N. N.　N. N.　N. N.　N. N.　N. N.　N. N.　N. N.
N. N.　N. N.　N. N.　N. N.　N. N.　N. N.　N. N.　N. N.　N. N.　N. N.
N. N.　N. N.　N. N.　N. N.　N. N.　N. N.　N. N.　N. N.　N. N.　N. N.
N. N.　N. N.　N. N.　N. N.　N. N.　N. N.　N. N.　N. N.　N. N.　N. N.
N. N.　N. N.　N. N.　N. N.　N. N.　N. N.　N. N.　N. N.　N. N.　N. N.
N. N.　N. N.　N. N.　N. N.　N. N.　N. N.　N. N.　N. N.　N. N.　N. N.
N. N.　N. N.　N. N.　N. N.　N. N.　N. N.　N. N.　N. N.　N. N.　N. N.
N. N.　N. N.　N. N.　N. N.　N. N.　N. N.　N. N.　N. N.　N. N.　N. N.
N. N.　N. N.　N. N.　N. N.　N. N.　N. N.　N. N.　N. N.　N. N.　N. N.
N. N.　N. N.　N. N.　N. N.　N. N.　N. N.　N. N.　N. N.　N. N.　N. N.
N. N.　N. N.　N. N.　N. N.　N. N.　N. N.　N. N.　N. N.　N. N.　N. N.
N. N.　N. N.　N. N.　N. N.　N. N.　N. N.　N. N.　N. N.　N. N.　N. N.
N. N.　N. N.　N. N.　N. N.　N. N.　N. N.　N. N.　N. N.　N. N.　N. N.
N. N.　N. N.　N. N.　N. N.　N. N.　N. N.　N. N.　N. N.　N. N.　N. N.
N. N.　N. N.　N. N.　N. N.　N. N.　N. N.　N. N.　N. N.　N. N.　N. N.
N. N.　N. N.　N. N.　N. N.　N. N.　N. N.　N. N.　N. N.　N. N.　N. N.
N. N.　N. N.　N. N.　N. N.　N. N.　N. N.　N. N.　N. N.　N. N.　N. N.
N. N.　N. N.　N. N.　N. N.　N. N.　N. N.　N. N.　N. N.　N. N.　N. N.
N. N.　N. N.　N. N.　N. N.　N. N.　N. N.　N. N.　N. N.　N. N.　N. N.
N. N.　N. N.　N. N.　N. N.　N. N.　N. N.　N. N.　N. N.　N. N.　N. N.
N. N.　N. N.　N. N.　N. N.　N. N.　N. N.　N. N.　N. N.　N. N.　N. N.
N. N.　N. N.　N. N.　N. N.　N. N.　N. N.　N. N.　N. N.　N. N.　N. N.

N. N.　N. N.　N. N.　N. N.　N. N.　N. N.　N. N.　N. N.　N. N.　N. N.

N. N.　N. N.　N. N.　N. N.　N. N.　N. N.　N. N.　N. N.　N. N.　N. N.

N. N.　N. N.　N. N.　N. N.　N. N.　N. N.　N. N.　N. N.　N. N.　N. N.

N. N.　N. N.　N. N.　N. N.　N. N.　N. N.　N. N.　N. N.　N. N.　N. N.

N. N.　N. N.　N. N.　N. N.　N. N.　N. N.　N. N.　N. N.　N. N.　N. N.

N. N.　N. N.　N. N.　N. N.　N. N.　N. N.　N. N.　N. N.　N. N.　N. N.

N. N.　N. N.　N. N.　N. N.　N. N.　N. N.　N. N.　N. N.　N. N.　N. N.

N. N.　N. N.　N. N.　N. N.　N. N.　N. N.　N. N.　N. N.　N. N.　N. N.

N. N.　N. N.　N. N.　N. N.　N. N.　N. N.　N. N.　N. N.　N. N.　N. N.

N. N.　N. N.　N. N.　N. N.　N. N.　N. N.　N. N.　N. N.　N. N.　N. N.

N. N.　N. N.　N. N.　N. N.　N. N.　N. N.　N. N.　N. N.　N. N.　N. N.

N. N.　N. N.　N. N.　N. N.　N. N.　N. N.　N. N.　N. N.　N. N.　N. N.

N. N.　N. N.　N. N.　N. N.　N. N.　N. N.　N. N.　N. N.　N. N.　N. N.

N. N.　N. N.　N. N.　N. N.　N. N.　N. N.　N. N.　N. N.　N. N.　N. N.

N. N.　N. N.　N. N.　N. N.　N. N.　N. N.　N. N.　N. N.　N. N.　N. N.

N. N.　N. N.　N. N.　N. N.　N. N.　N. N.　N. N.　N. N.　N. N.　N. N.

N. N.　N. N.　N. N.　N. N.　N. N.　N. N.　N. N.　N. N.　N. N.　N. N.

N. N.　N. N.　N. N.　N. N.　N. N.　N. N.　N. N.　N. N.　N. N.　N. N.

N. N.　N. N.　N. N.　N. N.　N. N.　N. N.　N. N.　N. N.　N. N.　N. N.

N. N.　N. N.　N. N.　N. N.　N. N.　N. N.　N. N.　N. N.　N. N.　N. N.

N. N.　N. N.　N. N.　N. N.　N. N.　N. N.　N. N.　N. N.　N. N.　N. N.

N. N.　N. N.　N. N.　N. N.　N. N.　N. N.　N. N.　N. N.　N. N.　N. N.

N. N.　N. N.　N. N.　N. N.　N. N.　N. N.　N. N.　N. N.　N. N.　N. N.

N. N.　N. N.　N. N.　N. N.　N. N.　N. N.　N. N.　N. N.　N. N.　N. N.

N. N.　N. N.　N. N.　N. N.　N. N.　N. N.　N. N.　N. N.　N. N.　N. N.

N. N.　N. N.　N. N.　N. N.　N. N.　N. N.　N. N.　N. N.　N. N.　N. N.

N. N.　N. N.　N. N.　N. N.　N. N.　N. N.　N. N.　N. N.　N. N.　N. N.

N. N.　N. N.　N. N.　N. N.　N. N.　N. N.　N. N.　N. N.　N. N.　N. N.

N. N.　N. N.　N. N.　N. N.　N. N.　N. N.　N. N.　N. N.　N. N.　N. N.

N. N.　N. N.　N. N.　N. N.　N. N.　N. N.　N. N.　N. N.　N. N.　N. N.

N. N.　N. N.　N. N.　N. N.　N. N.　N. N.　N. N.　N. N.　N. N.　N. N.

N. N.　N. N.　N. N.　N. N.　N. N.　N. N.　N. N.　N. N.　N. N.　N. N.

N. N.　N. N.　N. N.　N. N.　N. N.　N. N.　N. N.　N. N.　N. N.　N. N.

N. N.　N. N.　N. N.　N. N.　N. N.　N. N.　N. N.　N. N.　N. N.　N. N.

N. N.　N. N.　N. N.　N. N.　N. N.　N. N.　N. N.　N. N.　N. N.　N. N.

N. N.　N. N.　N. N.　N. N.　N. N.　N. N.　N. N.　N. N.　N. N.　N. N.

N. N. N. N. N. N. N. N. N. N. N. N. N. N. N. N. N. N. N. N.
N. N. N. N. N. N. N. N. N. N. N. N. N. N. N. N. N. N. N. N.
N. N. N. N. N. N. N. N. N. N. N. N. N. N. N. N. N. N. N. N.
N. N. N. N. N. N. N. N. N. N. N. N. N. N. N. N. N. N. N. N.
N. N. N. N. N. N. N. N. N. N. N. N. N. N. N. N. N. N. N. N.
N. N. N. N. N. N. N. N. N. N. N. N. N. N. N. N. N. N. N. N.
N. N. N. N. N. N. N. N. N. N. N. N. N. N. N. N. N. N. N. N.
N. N. N. N. N. N. N. N. N. N. N. N. N. N. N. N. N. N. N. N.
N. N. N. N. N. N. N. N. N. N. N. N. N. N. N. N. N. N. N. N.
N. N. N. N. N. N. N. N. N. N. N. N. N. N. N. N. N. N. N. N.
N. N. N. N. N. N. N. N. N. N. N. N. N. N. N. N. N. N. N. N.
N. N. N. N. N. N. N. N. N. N. N. N. N. N. N. N. N. N. N. N.
N. N. N. N. N. N. N. N. N. N. N. N. N. N. N. N. N. N. N. N.
N. N. N. N. N. N. N. N. N. N. N. N. N. N. N. N. N. N. N. N.
N. N. N. N. N. N. N. N. N. N. N. N. N. N. N. N. N. N. N. N.
N. N. N. N. N. N. N. N. N. N. N. N. N. N. N. N. N. N. N. N.
N. N. N. N. N. N. N. N. N. N. N. N. N. N. N. N. N. N. N. N.
N. N. N. N. N. N. N. N. N. N. N. N. N. N. N. N. N. N. N. N.
N. N. N. N. N. N. N. N. N. N. N. N. N. N. N. N. N. N. N. N.
N. N. N. N. N. N. N. N. N. N. N. N. N. N. N. N. N. N. N. N.
N. N. N. N. N. N. N. N. N. N. N. N. N. N. N. N. N. N. N. N.
N. N. N. N. N. N. N. N. N. N. N. N. N. N. N. N. N. N. N. N.
N. N. N. N. N. N. N. N. N. N. N. N. N. N. N. N. N. N. N. N.
N. N. N. N. N. N. N. N. N. N. N. N. N. N. N. N. N. N. N. N.
N. N. N. N. N. N. N. N. N. N. N. N. N. N. N. N. N. N. N. N.
N. N. N. N. N. N. N. N. N. N. N. N. N. N. N. N. N. N. N. N.
N. N. N. N. N. N. N. N. N. N. N. N. N. N. N. N. N. N. N. N.
N. N. N. N. N. N. N. N. N. N. N. N. N. N. N. N. N. N. N. N.
N. N. N. N. N. N. N. N. N. N. N. N. N. N. N. N. N. N. N. N.
N. N. N. N. N. N. N. N. N. N. N. N. N. N. N. N. N. N. N. N.
N. N. N. N. N. N. N. N. N. N. N. N. N. N. N. N. N. N. N. N.
N. N. N. N. N. N. N. N. N. N. N. N. N. N. N. N. N. N. N. N.
N. N. N. N. N. N. N. N. N. N. N. N. N. N. N. N. N. N. N. N.
N. N. N. N. N. N. N. N. N. N. N. N. N. N. N. N. N. N. N. N.
N. N. N. N. N. N. N. N. N. N. N. N. N. N. N. N. N. N. N. N.
N. N. N. N. N. N. N. N. N. N. N. N. N. N. N. N. N. N. N. N.
N. N. N. N. N. N. N. N. N. N. N. N. N. N. N. N. N. N. N. N.
N. N. N. N. N. N. N. N. N. N. N. N. N. N. N. N. N. N. N. N.
N. N. N. N. N. N. N. N. N. N. N. N. N. N. N. N. N. N. N. N.
N. N. N. N. N. N. N. N. N. N. N. N. N. N. N. N. N. N. N. N.
N. N. N. N. N. N. N. N. N. N. N. N. N. N. N. N. N. N. N. N.
N. N. N. N. N. N. N. N. N. N. N. N. N. N. N. N. N. N. N. N.

N. N. N. N. N. N. N. N. N. N. N. N. N. N. N. N. N. N. N. N.
N. N. N. N. N. N. N. N. N. N. N. N. N. N. N. N. N. N. N. N.
N. N. N. N. N. N. N. N. N. N. N. N. N. N. N. N. N. N. N. N.
N. N. N. N. N. N. N. N. N. N. N. N. N. N. N. N. N. N. N. N.
N. N. N. N. N. N. N. N. N. N. N. N. N. N. N. N. N. N. N. N.
N. N. N. N. N. N. N. N. N. N. N. N. N. N. N. N. N. N. N. N.
N. N. N. N. N. N. N. N. N. N. N. N. N. N. N. N. N. N. N. N.
N. N. N. N. N. N. N. N. N. N. N. N. N. N. N. N. N. N. N. N.
N. N. N. N. N. N. N. N. N. N. N. N. N. N. N. N. N. N. N. N.
N. N. N. N. N. N. N. N. N. N. N. N. N. N. N. N. N. N. N. N.
N. N. N. N. N. N. N. N. N. N. N. N. N. N. N. N. N. N. N. N.
N. N. N. N. N. N. N. N. N. N. N. N. N. N. N. N. N. N. N. N.
N. N. N. N. N. N. N. N. N. N. N. N. N. N. N. N. N. N. N. N.
N. N. N. N. N. N. N. N. N. N. N. N. N. N. N. N. N. N. N. N.
N. N. N. N. N. N. N. N. N. N. N. N. N. N. N. N. N. N. N. N.
N. N. N. N. N. N. N. N. N. N. N. N. N. N. N. N. N. N. N. N.
N. N. N. N. N. N. N. N. N. N. N. N. N. N. N. N. N. N. N. N.
N. N. N. N. N. N. N. N. N. N. N. N. N. N. N. N. N. N. N. N.
N. N. N. N. N. N. N. N. N. N. N. N. N. N. N. N. N. N. N. N.
N. N. N. N. N. N. N. N. N. N. N. N. N. N. N. N. N. N. N. N.
N. N. N. N. N. N. N. N. N. N. N. N. N. N. N. N. N. N. N. N.
N. N. N. N. N. N. N. N. N. N. N. N. N. N. N. N. N. N. N. N.
N. N. N. N. N. N. N. N. N. N. N. N. N. N. N. N. N. N. N. N.
N. N. N. N. N. N. N. N. N. N. N. N. N. N. N. N. N. N. N. N.
N. N. N. N. N. N. N. N. N. N. N. N. N. N. N. N. N. N. N. N.
N. N. N. N. N. N. N. N. N. N. N. N. N. N. N. N. N. N. N. N.
N. N. N. N. N. N. N. N. N. N. N. N. N. N. N. N. N. N. N. N.
N. N. N. N. N. N. N. N. N. N. N. N. N. N. N. N. N. N. N. N.
N. N. N. N. N. N. N. N. N. N. N. N. N. N. N. N. N. N. N. N.
N. N. N. N. N. N. N. N. N. N. N. N. N. N. N. N. N. N. N. N.
N. N. N. N. N. N. N. N. N. N. N. N. N. N. N. N. N. N. N. N.
N. N. N. N. N. N. N. N. N. N. N. N. N. N. N. N. N. N. N. N.
N. N. N. N. N. N. N. N. N. N. N. N. N. N. N. N. N. N. N. N.
N. N. N. N. N. N. N. N. N. N. N. N. N. N. N. N. N. N. N. N.
N. N. N. N. N. N. N. N. N. N. N. N. N. N. N. N. N. N. N. N.
N. N. N. N. N. N. N. N. N. N. N. N. N. N. N. N. N. N. N. N.
N. N. N. N. N. N. N. N. N. N. N. N. N. N. N. N. N. N. N. N.
N. N. N. N. N. N. N. N. N. N. N. N. N. N. N. N. N. N. N. N.
N. N. N. N. N. N. N. N. N. N. N. N. N. N. N. N. N. N. N. N.

N. N.	N. N.	N. N.	N. N.	N. N.	N. N.	N. N.	N. N.	N. N.	N. N.
N. N.	N. N.	N. N.	N. N.	N. N.	N. N.	N. N.	N. N.	N. N.	N. N.
N. N.	N. N.	N. N.	N. N.	N. N.	N. N.	N. N.	N. N.	N. N.	N. N.
N. N.	N. N.	N. N.	N. N.	N. N.	N. N.	N. N.	N. N.	N. N.	N. N.
N. N.	N. N.	N. N.	N. N.	N. N.	N. N.	N. N.	N. N.	N. N.	N. N.
N. N.	N. N.	N. N.	N. N.	N. N.	N. N.	N. N.	N. N.	N. N.	N. N.
N. N.	N. N.	N. N.	N. N.	N. N.	N. N.	N. N.	N. N.	N. N.	N. N.
N. N.	N. N.	N. N.	N. N.	N. N.	N. N.	N. N.	N. N.	N. N.	N. N.
N. N.	N. N.	N. N.	N. N.	N. N.	N. N.	N. N.	N. N.	N. N.	N. N.
N. N.	N. N.	N. N.	N. N.	N. N.	N. N.	N. N.	N. N.	N. N.	N. N.
N. N.	N. N.	N. N.	N. N.	N. N.	N. N.	N. N.	N. N.	N. N.	N. N.
N. N.	N. N.	N. N.	N. N.	N. N.	N. N.	N. N.	N. N.	N. N.	N. N.
N. N.	N. N.	N. N.	N. N.	N. N.	N. N.	N. N.	N. N.	N. N.	N. N.
N. N.	N. N.	N. N.	N. N.	N. N.	N. N.	N. N.	N. N.	N. N.	N. N.
N. N.	N. N.	N. N.	N. N.	N. N.	N. N.	N. N.	N. N.	N. N.	N. N.
N. N.	N. N.	N. N.	N. N.	N. N.	N. N.	N. N.	N. N.	N. N.	N. N.
N. N.	N. N.	N. N.	N. N.	N. N.	N. N.	N. N.	N. N.	N. N.	N. N.
N. N.	N. N.	N. N.	N. N.	N. N.	N. N.	N. N.	N. N.	N. N.	N. N.
N. N.	N. N.	N. N.	N. N.	N. N.	N. N.	N. N.	N. N.	N. N.	N. N.
N. N.	N. N.	N. N.	N. N.	N. N.	N. N.	N. N.	N. N.	N. N.	N. N.
N. N.	N. N.	N. N.	N. N.	N. N.	N. N.	N. N.	N. N.	N. N.	N. N.
N. N.	N. N.	N. N.	N. N.	N. N.	N. N.	N. N.	N. N.	N. N.	N. N.
N. N.	N. N.	N. N.	N. N.	N. N.	N. N.	N. N.	N. N.	N. N.	N. N.
N. N.	N. N.	N. N.	N. N.	N. N.	N. N.	N. N.	N. N.	N. N.	N. N.
N. N.	N. N.	N. N.	N. N.	N. N.	N. N.	N. N.	N. N.	N. N.	N. N.
N. N.	N. N.	N. N.	N. N.	N. N.	N. N.	N. N.	N. N.	N. N.	N. N.
N. N.	N. N.	N. N.	N. N.	N. N.	N. N.	N. N.	N. N.	N. N.	N. N.
N. N.	N. N.	N. N.	N. N.	N. N.	N. N.	N. N.	N. N.	N. N.	N. N.
N. N.	N. N.	N. N.	N. N.	N. N.	N. N.	N. N.	N. N.	N. N.	N. N.
N. N.	N. N.	N. N.	N. N.	N. N.	N. N.	N. N.	N. N.	N. N.	N. N.
N. N.	N. N.	N. N.	N. N.	N. N.	N. N.	N. N.	N. N.	N. N.	N. N.
N. N.	N. N.	N. N.	N. N.	N. N.	N. N.	N. N.	N. N.	N. N.	N. N.
N. N.	N. N.	N. N.	N. N.	N. N.	N. N.	N. N.	N. N.	N. N.	N. N.
N. N.	N. N.	N. N.	N. N.	N. N.	N. N.	N. N.	N. N.	N. N.	N. N.
N. N.	N. N.	N. N.	N. N.	N. N.	N. N.	N. N.	N. N.	N. N.	N. N.
N. N.	N. N.	N. N.	N. N.	N. N.	N. N.	N. N.	N. N.	N. N.	N. N.
N. N.	N. N.	N. N.	N. N.	N. N.	N. N.	N. N.	N. N.	N. N.	N. N.
N. N.	N. N.	N. N.	N. N.	N. N.	N. N.	N. N.	N. N.	N. N.	N. N.
N. N.	N. N.	N. N.	N. N.	N. N.	N. N.	N. N.	N. N.	N. N.	N. N.
N. N.	N. N.	N. N.	N. N.	N. N.	N. N.	N. N.	N. N.	N. N.	N. N.

N. N.   N. N.   N. N.   N. N.   N. N.   N. N.   N. N.   N. N.   N. N.   N. N.

N. N.   N. N.   N. N.   N. N.   N. N.   N. N.   N. N.   N. N.   N. N.   N. N.

N. N.   N. N.   N. N.   N. N.   N. N.   N. N.   N. N.   N. N.   N. N.   N. N.

N. N.   N. N.   N. N.   N. N.   N. N.   N. N.   N. N.   N. N.   N. N.   N. N.

N. N.   N. N.   N. N.   N. N.   N. N.   N. N.   N. N.   N. N.   N. N.   N. N.

N. N.   N. N.   N. N.   N. N.   N. N.   N. N.   N. N.   N. N.   N. N.   N. N.

N. N.   N. N.   N. N.   N. N.   N. N.   N. N.   N. N.   N. N.   N. N.   N. N.

N. N.   N. N.   N. N.   N. N.   N. N.   N. N.   N. N.   N. N.   N. N.   N. N.

N. N.   N. N.   N. N.   N. N.   N. N.   N. N.   N. N.   N. N.   N. N.   N. N.

N. N.   N. N.   N. N.   N. N.   N. N.   N. N.   N. N.   N. N.   N. N.   N. N.

N. N.   N. N.   N. N.   N. N.   N. N.   N. N.   N. N.   N. N.   N. N.   N. N.

N. N.   N. N.   N. N.   N. N.   N. N.   N. N.   N. N.   N. N.   N. N.   N. N.

N. N.   N. N.   N. N.   N. N.   N. N.   N. N.   N. N.   N. N.   N. N.   N. N.

N. N.   N. N.   N. N.   N. N.   N. N.   N. N.   N. N.   N. N.   N. N.   N. N.

N. N.   N. N.   N. N.   N. N.   N. N.   N. N.   N. N.   N. N.   N. N.   N. N.

N. N.   N. N.   N. N.   N. N.   N. N.   N. N.   N. N.   N. N.   N. N.   N. N.

N. N.   N. N.   N. N.   N. N.   N. N.   N. N.   N. N.   N. N.   N. N.   N. N.

N. N.   N. N.   N. N.   N. N.   N. N.   N. N.   N. N.   N. N.   N. N.   N. N.

N. N.   N. N.   N. N.   N. N.   N. N.   N. N.   N. N.   N. N.   N. N.   N. N.

N. N.   N. N.   N. N.   N. N.   N. N.   N. N.   N. N.   N. N.   N. N.   N. N.

N. N.   N. N.   N. N.   N. N.   N. N.   N. N.   N. N.   N. N.   N. N.   N. N.

N. N.   N. N.   N. N.   N. N.   N. N.   N. N.   N. N.   N. N.   N. N.   N. N.

N. N.   N. N.   N. N.   N. N.   N. N.   N. N.   N. N.   N. N.   N. N.   N. N.

N. N.   N. N.   N. N.   N. N.   N. N.   N. N.   N. N.   N. N.   N. N.   N. N.

N. N.   N. N.   N. N.   N. N.   N. N.   N. N.   N. N.   N. N.   N. N.   N. N.

N. N.   N. N.   N. N.   N. N.   N. N.   N. N.   N. N.   N. N.   N. N.   N. N.

N. N.   N. N.   N. N.   N. N.   N. N.   N. N.   N. N.   N. N.   N. N.   N. N.

N. N.   N. N.   N. N.   N. N.   N. N.   N. N.   N. N.   N. N.   N. N.   N. N.

N. N.   N. N.   N. N.   N. N.   N. N.   N. N.   N. N.   N. N.   N. N.   N. N.

N. N.   N. N.   N. N.   N. N.   N. N.   N. N.   N. N.   N. N.   N. N.   N. N.

N. N.   N. N.   N. N.   N. N.   N. N.   N. N.   N. N.   N. N.   N. N.   N. N.

N. N.   N. N.   N. N.   N. N.   N. N.   N. N.   N. N.   N. N.   N. N.   N. N.

N. N.   N. N.   N. N.   N. N.   N. N.   N. N.   N. N.   N. N.   N. N.   N. N.

N. N.   N. N.   N. N.   N. N.   N. N.   N. N.   N. N.   N. N.   N. N.   N. N.

N. N.   N. N.   N. N.   N. N.   N. N.   N. N.   N. N.   N. N.   N. N.   N. N.

N. N.   N. N.   N. N.   N. N.   N. N.   N. N.   N. N.   N. N.   N. N.   N. N.

N. N.   N. N.   N. N.   N. N.   N. N.   N. N.   N. N.   N. N.   N. N.   N. N.

N. N.   N. N.   N. N.   N. N.   N. N.   N. N.   N. N.   N. N.   N. N.   N. N.

N. N.   N. N.   N. N.   N. N.   N. N.   N. N.   N. N.   N. N.   N. N.   N. N.

N. N.   N. N.   N. N.   N. N.   N. N.   N. N.   N. N.   N. N.   N. N.   N. N.

N. N.   N. N.   N. N.   N. N.   N. N.   N. N.   N. N.   N. N.   N. N.   N. N.

N. N.   N. N.   N. N.   N. N.   N. N.   N. N.   N. N.   N. N.   N. N.   N. N.

N. N.   N. N.   N. N.   N. N.   N. N.   N. N.   N. N.   N. N.   N. N.   N. N.

N. N.   N. N.   N. N.   N. N.   N. N.   N. N.   N. N.   N. N.   N. N.   N. N.

N. N.   N. N.   N. N.   N. N.   N. N.   N. N.   N. N.   N. N.   N. N.   N. N.

N. N.   N. N.   N. N.   N. N.   N. N.   N. N.   N. N.   N. N.   N. N.   N. N.

N. N.   N. N.   N. N.   N. N.   N. N.   N. N.   N. N.   N. N.   N. N.   N. N.

N. N.   N. N.   N. N.   N. N.   N. N.   N. N.   N. N.   N. N.   N. N.   N. N.

N. N.   N. N.   N. N.   N. N.   N. N.   N. N.   N. N.   N. N.   N. N.   N. N.

N. N.   N. N.   N. N.   N. N.   N. N.   N. N.   N. N.   N. N.   N. N.   N. N.

N. N.   N. N.   N. N.   N. N.   N. N.   N. N.   N. N.   N. N.   N. N.   N. N.

N. N.   N. N.   N. N.   N. N.   N. N.   N. N.   N. N.   N. N.   N. N.   N. N.

N. N.   N. N.   N. N.   N. N.   N. N.   N. N.   N. N.   N. N.   N. N.   N. N.

N. N.   N. N.   N. N.   N. N.   N. N.   N. N.   N. N.   N. N.   N. N.   N. N.

N. N.   N. N.   N. N.   N. N.   N. N.   N. N.   N. N.   N. N.   N. N.   N. N.

N. N.   N. N.   N. N.   N. N.   N. N.   N. N.   N. N.   N. N.   N. N.   N. N.

N. N.   N. N.   N. N.   N. N.   N. N.   N. N.   N. N.   N. N.   N. N.   N. N.

N. N.   N. N.   N. N.   N. N.   N. N.   N. N.   N. N.   N. N.   N. N.   N. N.

N. N.   N. N.   N. N.   N. N.   N. N.   N. N.   N. N.   N. N.   N. N.   N. N.

N. N.   N. N.   N. N.   N. N.   N. N.   N. N.   N. N.   N. N.   N. N.   N. N.

N. N.   N. N.   N. N.   N. N.   N. N.   N. N.   N. N.   N. N.   N. N.   N. N.

N. N.   N. N.   N. N.   N. N.   N. N.   N. N.   N. N.   N. N.   N. N.   N. N.

N. N.   N. N.   N. N.   N. N.   N. N.   N. N.   N. N.   N. N.   N. N.   N. N.

N. N.   N. N.   N. N.   N. N.   N. N.   N. N.   N. N.   N. N.   N. N.   N. N.

N. N.   N. N.   N. N.   N. N.   N. N.   N. N.   N. N.   N. N.   N. N.   N. N.

N. N.   N. N.   N. N.   N. N.   N. N.   N. N.   N. N.   N. N.   N. N.   N. N.

N. N.   N. N.   N. N.   N. N.   N. N.   N. N.   N. N.   N. N.   N. N.   N. N.

N. N.   N. N.   N. N.   N. N.   N. N.   N. N.   N. N.   N. N.   N. N.

N. N.   N. N.   N. N.   N. N.   N. N.   N. N.   N. N.   N. N.   N. N.

N. N.   N. N.   N. N.   N. N.   N. N.   N. N.   N. N.   N. N.   N. N.

N. N.   N. N.   N. N.   N. N.   N. N.   N. N.   N. N.   N. N.   N. N.

N. N.   N. N.   N. N.   N. N.   N. N.   N. N.   N. N.   N. N.   N. N.

N. N.   N. N.   N. N.   N. N.   N. N.   N. N.   N. N.   N. N.   N. N.

N. N.   N. N.   N. N.   N. N.   N. N.   N. N.   N. N.   N. N.   N. N.

N. N.   N. N.   N. N.   N. N.   N. N.   N. N.   N. N.   N. N.   N. N.

N. N.   N. N.   N. N.   N. N.   N. N.   N. N.   N. N.   N. N.   N. N.

N. N.   N. N.   N. N.   N. N.   N. N.   N. N.   N. N.   N. N.   N. N.

N. N.   N. N.   N. N.   N. N.   N. N.   N. N.   N. N.   N. N.   N. N.

N. N.   N. N.   N. N.   N. N.   N. N.   N. N.   N. N.   N. N.   N. N.

N. N.   N. N.   N. N.   N. N.   N. N.   N. N.   N. N.   N. N.   N. N.

N. N.   N. N.   N. N.   N. N.   N. N.   N. N.   N. N.   N. N.   N. N.

N. N.   N. N.   N. N.   N. N.   N. N.   N. N.   N. N.   N. N.   N. N.

N. N.   N. N.   N. N.   N. N.   N. N.   N. N.   N. N.   N. N.   N. N.

N. N.   N. N.   N. N.   N. N.   N. N.   N. N.   N. N.   N. N.   N. N.

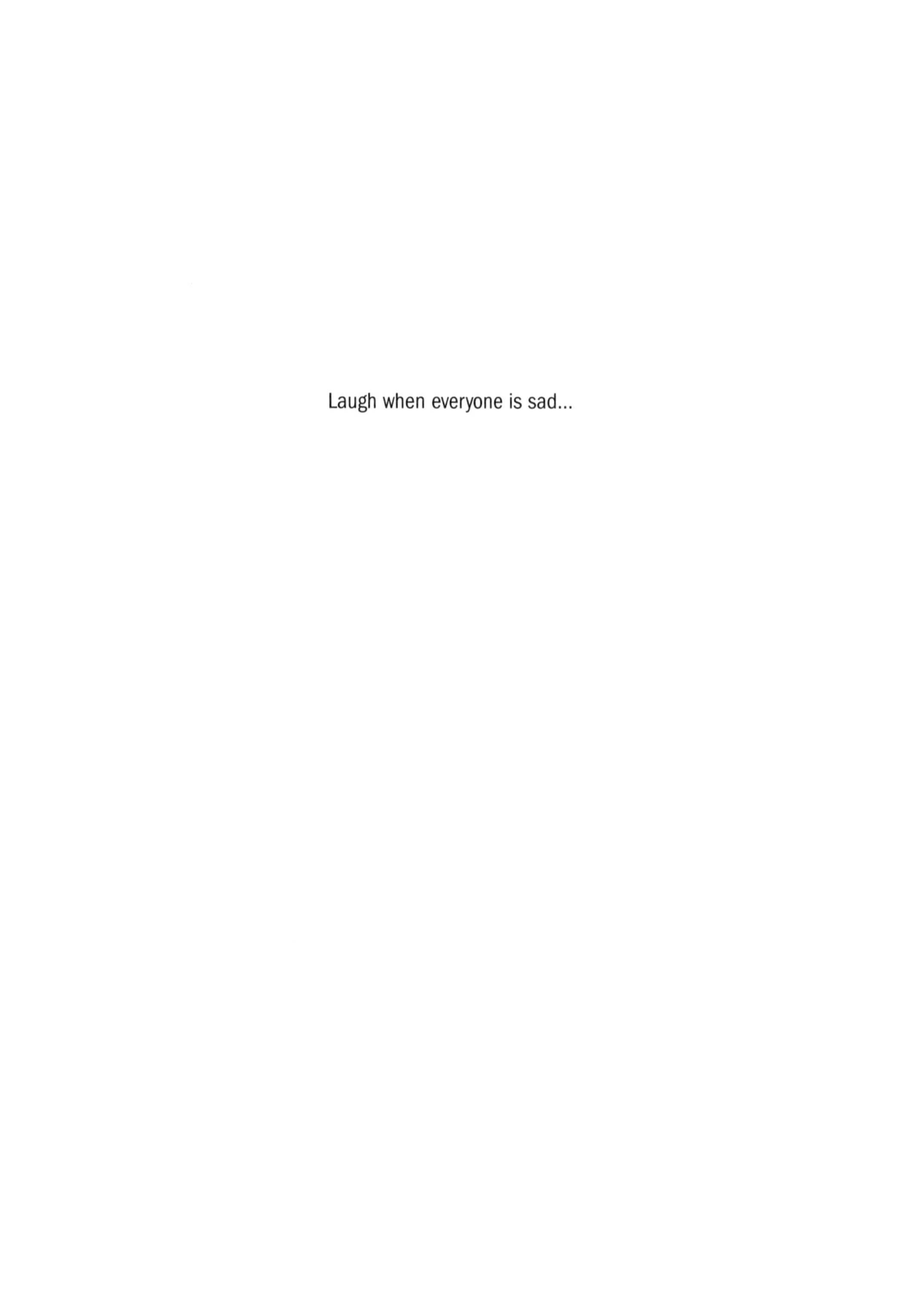

Laugh when everyone is sad...

Preliminary results:

YES receives 51.3%

- The independent staff for the YES campaign counted a total of 2,022,579 votes, conferring upon YES 50.3% of the vote
- The NO campaign declared victory with 60.1%
- The president of the Free Elections Committee, CEL, has called on citizens to remain calm until final results are delivered

*HE RAN ALONE AND
CAME IN SECOND!*

COUNTRY: CHILE

wt ageanrdssuid
ujzammgneia
ioavono njov
iadg roarcarci
uacsaurbh n
rioonrgefeaap jsro
grr somooeuizabdri
mdyfenaoroalm
dcarcl iaorro
rediso gzei

AFBRGHJKIYHBNMVCXZSDGUTESAUGUSTOPINOCHETDXSKCF
GBNUEAMANUELCONTRERASDCVBGFDHYTFWWSADFGHJGFC
PEDROESPINOZASDCVBGFDRTEWSAQFHKJHRTYIGRESCACRT
SAEFGYUIOHGVEDUARDOITURRIAGANFCVBSEXCRTYUIOMAR
CELOMORENBRITOFSEDCVBHUITASDCVBDSEERCDYDEASRT
UIOPVMIGUELKRASSNOFFRDESAQWERTFVBUENUIFDRADVO
DLANIERMENADCSVBYUIOOHURTGFDECVBNMUDSEISTUOPG
BJILKDFHUMBERTOGORDONASDEWQZXCFTUIOSEDERTBGSE
UIOMONICAMADARIAGAWASRFVBGTYUIOPLITEDTGSERGIOO
NOFREJARPASERFCDSAQUIOPLHTUNIOFDRTYFBHIKLORTGB
NDESWASERGIOFERNANDEZSAEDRTYUIOPHGDSCVBUERTGD
CSAZOSVALDOROMOESAWQTUIPGHNBDSADERTUIGVHSRPLJ
GDSFERNANDOTORRESDESAWRTCVHIOPLGBSERGIOARREDO
NDOEASWDRTHVDSQTUIGBCSDFHYUIMDFERJULIOALVAROCO
RBALANDFEQASCVGHUIOPHGFDSADERGFDSACVBUOEDNSWQ
ASDERMANFREDOMAYOLESWASXCVREDSADERTUGFDROIUTR
JAIMEGUZMANDEASQWRTYUNGFRTYUIOPLKGTREDCFSWEPE
DROASXINORAWALBERTOCARDEMILTREDCVBNUIJGFDESAWE
RFSERGIOARELLANOSTSRXRTGADRFUIPLFCDRHUGOSALASW
ENZELESAWRTUGFDERTYUIOCARLOSHERRERAEASDRTYFCVB
FDWAQWERTGHYUIOPFDADIODRTCVBNMGERARDOGODOYGA
RCIASWAQWERFCAHUIOPFCEGTYNBDSACGHJUIBASCLAYZAPATAREY
ESDXZAUJGFCBYUIODCVIANELVALDIVIESOCERVANT
ESOPGTFSERTGVBNASDCVFRJULIOLOPEZBLANCOESAQUTGB
UIOPLKGDSERTVDCLAUDIOSANCHEZSQAERTUIOPLOKDAERG
UIYFDSCGTEAADEDTUPLOHBVDUIRDAXCVFEQADETUPABLO
HONORATOFCAHUIOPEASQWRTYURESDEGTREDCVBERTUHNK

"We didn't kill anyone who wasn't a terrorist"

"I never forced anyone to kill or gave any order to kill"

"No order to kill exists in the Chilean Army"

"My hands aren't stained with blood"

"I fulfilled my mission according to the instructions and orders I was given"

"I was just following orders!"

"I was given orders that corresponded to my job...
and I tried to complete those orders to the best of my ability"

"I'm proud of what was done"

Murder
Aggravated murder
Kidnapping with murder
Aggravated kidnapping
Forced disappearance
Double homicide
Illicit association
Attempted homicide
Aggravated double homicide
Kidnapping and disappearance
Kidnapping and aggravated homicide
Aggravated kidnapping and result of death

4 years

6 years

6 years

10 years

10 years

10 years

18 years

116 years and 11 days

275 years

360 years

life sentence

life sentence

back-to-back life sentences

four life sentences

dementia
mixed dementia
Alzheimer's disease
vascular dementia
multifactorial dementia
severe mental deterioration
progressive and irreversible vascular dementia
progressive and incurable subcortical dementia
partial sphincter control
inability to dress or clean oneself

My Lords,

Charges 1, 2 and 5:

conspiracy to torture between 1 January 1972 and 20 September 1973
and between 1 August 1973 and 1 January 1990;

Charge 3:

conspiracy to take hostages between 1 August 1973 and 1 January 1990;

Charge 4:

conspiracy to torture in furtherance of which murder was committed in
various countries including Italy, France, Spain and Portugal, between
1 January 1972 and 1 January 1990.

Charges 6 and 8:

torture between 1 August 1973 and 8 August 1973
and on 11 September 1973.

Charges 9 and 12:

conspiracy to murder in Spain between 1 January 1975 and 31 December
1976 and in Italy on 6 October 1975.

Charges 10 and 11:

attempted murder in Italy on 6 October 1975.

Charges 13–29; and 31–32:

torture on various occasions between
11 September 1973 and May 1977.

Charge 30:

torture on 24 June 1989.

I turn then to consider which of those charges are extradition crimes.

Senator Pinochet is not immune
Senator Pinochet is not immune
Senator Pinochet is not immune
Senator Pinochet is not immune
Senator Pinochet is not immune
Senator Pinochet is not immune
Senator Pinochet is not immune
Senator Pinochet is not immune
Senator Pinochet is not immune
Senator Pinochet is not immune
Senator Pinochet is not immune
Senator Pinochet is not immune
Senator Pinochet is not immune
Senator Pinochet is not immune
Senator Pinochet is not immune
Senator Pinochet is not immune
Senator Pinochet is not immune
Senator Pinochet is not immune
Senator Pinochet is not immune
Senator Pinochet is not immune
Senator Pinochet is not immune
Senator Pinochet is not immune
Senator Pinochet is not immune
Senator Pinochet is not immune
Senator Pinochet is not immune
Senator Pinochet is not immune
Senator Pinochet is not immune
Senator Pinochet is not immune
Senator Pinochet is not immune
Senator Pinochet is not immune

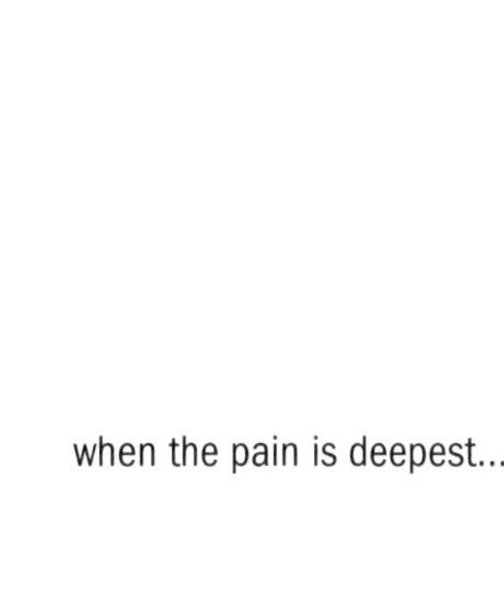

when the pain is deepest...

when the soul is wounded...

it is time...

to gather the ranks...

in silence...

and take control...

of the powers of the State!

[5] Convention against Torture and Other Cruel, Inhuman or Degrading Treatment or Punishment (UN), Art. 1.1, ratified by Chile with Decree No. 808, published on November 26, 1988.

[6] Inter-American Convention to Prevent and Punish Torture (OAS), Art. 2, ratified by Chile with Decree No. 809, published on November 26, 1988.

a) Killed by State agents or persons at their command:

    - in war tribunals   xx

    - from excessive force during protests   xx

    - during alleged escape attempts   xxx

    - other executions and deaths by torture   xxx

              Subtotal   xxxx

b) Arrested by State agents and disappeared   xxx

c) Killed in attacks committed by civilians under political pretexts _________ xx

Total   xxxx

1973	661 boys and girls	61.2%
1974–77	236 boys	21.8%
1978–1990	183 boys	17%

1973	517	719	0	1236
1974	244	81	4	329
1975	88	28	5	121
1976	123	9	16	148
1977	8	12	15	35
1978	7	2	8	17
1979	10	3	1	14
1980	11	4	0	15
1981	23	12	2	37
1982	9	0	0	9
1983	67	15	0	82
1984	51	22	0	73
1985	38	10	0	48
1986	43	4	0	47
1987	31	3	0	34
1988	16	11	0	27
1989	19	6	0	25
1990	1	0	0	1
	1306	941	51	2298

Several recommendations for restitution and symbolic reparations:

Oops! Google Chrome could not find
        www.comisionprisionpoliticaytortura.cl.

Try reloading: www.comisionprisionpoliticaytortura.gov.cl

Additional suggestions:
· Search on Google:

                              comisionprisonpoliticaytortura cl

http://www.red.gov.cl/info

Government
of Chile

The requested object does not exist
State Connectivity Network (SCN)

THE LAST ONE (WHO IS ALSO THE FIRST ONE)

*At dawn on September 3rd, 2005, according to anonymous witness statements, **José Gerardo Huenante Huenante**, 16 years old, of Mapuche origin, confronted police on Vicuña Mackenna Avenue in Puerto Montt's Mirasol neighborhood, where he was thrown into patrol car No. 1375, belonging to the 5th Precinct of Puerto Montt. His whereabouts have been unknown ever since.*

people only speak of these things in Chile...

Grandpa,

how did we become such a great country?

"Attention post one": Orders given to soldiers on September 11, 1973, recorded by an anonymous ham radio user. In 1998, journalist Patricia Verdugo published the transcriptions of the full recording, along with a CD, in *Interferencia Secreta* (*Secret Interference*).

"NATIONAL STADIUM SCOREBOARD": Results of the 1974 World Cup qualifying playoff match between Chile and the Soviet Union, played on November 21, 1973. Although the Soviet Union did not arrive for the match, Chile still organized the game. In a full stadium with no rival, the Chilean team kicked off the ball, made a few plays, and scored in an empty goal area, later known as the "goal of infamy."

"EXTERMINATED LIKE RATS": Headline published on July 24, 1975, by the daily *La Segunda*, referring to what is known as the Colombo Operation, in which the National Intelligence Directorate (DINA) assassinated 119 opponents of the dictatorship. The newspaper article claims that 59 members of the Revolutionary Left Movement (MIR) were killed in the operation, setting a precedent for media complicity during this period.

"Envelope containing checkbooks": Personal belongings of Spanish Diplomat Carmelo Soria, found at his office in Santiago. A member of the United Nations Economic Commission for Latin America and the Caribbean, Soria was killed by DINA agents in Operation Condor.

"SEPTEMBER 21, 1976": Taken from Gerald Ford's agenda.

"SPEECH AT CHACARILLAS": An event organized on July 9, 1977, to commemorate the Battle of La Concepción. In his speech, Augusto Pinochet honored 77 young professionals (representing the 77 martyrs of La Concepción), many of whom are to this day public figures, including politicians, journalists, athletes, and comedians.

"25/11 pinochet's birthday": Every November 25 during the dictatorship, the Chilean military band would celebrate Pinochet's birthday by playing his favorite songs outside his house. The form of this poem is based on a text from Heimrad Bäcker's *Transcript*.

"1810 CHILE 1973": Plaque in the main hall of the Diego Portales building, headquarters of the military junta directly following the coup d'état of September 11, 1973. The building, constructed under Allende's government to host the third conference of the United Nations Conference on Trade and Development, was renamed by the junta.

10-peso coin: Minted in 1976 and again in 1981, the coin displays a winged woman breaking her shackles, the word "Freedom," and the date of the coup d'état.

"National Plebiscite": In 1980, a national plebiscite was held to validate a new constitution for Chile, authored primarily by Jaime Guzmán.

"the dead man…": Falsified suicide note found next to Alegría Mundaca's body in his home in Valparaíso. In the letter, Alegría, a 41-year-old carpenter, confesses to having killed union leader Tucapel Jiménez. Later, it was discovered that Alegría's suicide was a government cover-up of the Jiménez assassination.

"Keep standing — 24 hours": Edgar Benjamín Cevallos Jones, a Chilean Air force Colonel using the alias "Inspector Cabezas," placed this sign on detainees to indicate that they should not be allowed to sit or rest for an entire day.

"AGA, CC, CNI…": State intelligence agencies involved in the persecution, kidnapping, torture, execution, and disappearance of political opponents or suspected dissidents during Pinochet's dictatorship. The National Intelligence Directorate (DINA) and later the National Information Center (CNI) were notorious for committing human rights violations.

"El Mamo": Nickname for Manuel Contreras, director of the DINA from 1973–1977. All the nicknames on this page correspond to torturers.

"everything seen heard": Pact of silence between military and civil perpetrators promising to never reveal information in regard to the disappeared victims of the dictatorship.

"I shoot or you shoot?": Slogan from a contest on *Sábado Gigante*, a game show hosted by Mario Kreutzberger, known by his stage name Don Francisco. The show aired in Chile from 1962–1986, after which Kreutzberger and the show relocated to Miami, Florida.

"(sound of a telegraph)": Transcription of two radio broadcasts reporting the discovery of three bodies with their throats slit near the Santiago airport. They were the bodies of Communist Party members Santiago Nattino, Manuel Guerrero, and José Manuel Parada. The case, known as "Caso Degollados," caused a political scandal in 1985.

"Pisagua Jail House…": Detention and torture centers. The Sexy Blindfold (La Venda Sexy), a two-story house located in Santiago, was infamous for the sexual assault of prisoners.

"N.N.": Initials used to indicate an unidentified corpse, taken from the Latin nomen nescio. Patio 29 in Santiago's General Cemetery is a mass grave site which the military used to bury unidentified bodies of executed political prisoners. Today, the area is preserved as a site of memory.

"Laugh when everyone is sad": Lyrics from the theme song of *Jappening con Ja*, a comedy TV show which aired from 1978–1989. Television played a fundamental role during the dictatorship, diverting attention from social and political issues or mitigating their impact.

"Preliminary results": On October 5, 1988, in the midst of international pressure for Pinochet to step down, a national referendum was held to determine if the dictatorship should continue. During the referendum, the junta did not want to recognize the possibility of the end of the dictatorship, and so projected YES in the news for all partial results. At the end of the day, however, the NO option received the majority vote, initiating the transition to a democratic government.

"HE RAN ALONE AND CAME IN SECOND!": Headline from the October 11, 1988 edition of left-wing newspaper *Fortín Mapocho*, announcing Pinochet's loss in the national referendum. The headline was written by Alberto "Gato" Gamboa.

"wt ageanrdssuid": Scrambled letters of the names of civilian collaborators of the dictatorship, many of whom are still active in politics.

"My Lords": From the rulings of the UK Parliament's House of Lords regarding the extradition of Augusto Pinochet in 1999.

"when the pain is deepest": Excerpt of a speech given by Pinochet's son, Augusto Pinochet Hiriart, after his father's arrest in London in October of 1998.

REMNANTS OF CHILE: BRINGING *11* INTO ENGLISH

*past horrors give us a language, or
a basis on which to create a new
language, to define new disasters.*
—Edwidge Danticat

In *The Truce*, Primo Levi recalls a 3-year-old Auschwitz prisoner whose speech is limited to one unintelligible word, pronounced *mass-klo* or *matisklo*. Hurbinek, as the other prisoners name him, an orphan without language or nation, dies in the first days of March 1945, leaving nothing of his existence but this brief memory in Levi's testimonial novel. Years later, philosopher Giorgio Agamben returns to this episode to illustrate the paradox of testimony, which he calls "the disjunction between two impossibilities of bearing witness," for the deceased cannot tell their story and survivors can only tell one version. In this sense, Hurbinek's noises represent the embryonic utterances of a language seeking to denounce the horrors of genocide, but which must accept the inadequacy of words, the impossibility of testimonial perspective. Carlos Soto Román's *11* begins from a similar premise by attempting to document the fractured memory of one of South America's most notorious dictatorships.

The title of this book carries the weight of nearly half a century concentrated in one day: September 11, 1973, when Augusto Pinochet led a military coup to oust the democratically elected government of Salvador Allende, inaugurating a 17-year dictatorship that upended Chile's political and social system. Whether we pronounce the title "eleven" or "once" in Spanish, this number embodies much more than some quantifiable thing. Its symbolic burden still presses deep into Chile's social fibers, after only partial reconciliations and pacts of silence with perpetrators. September 11 is a fault line in the country's recent history, representing a ground zero of trauma for some and a patriotic triumph for others; while yet others view the military intervention as a necessary evil and profess turning the page on history.

Though Allende's Popular Unity coalition sought to bring about profound social transformations, Pinochet was the one to orchestrate a neoliberal revolution and usher Chile into the 21st century with economic stability but widespread inequalities. The antipoet Nicanor Parra once illustrated the paradox of the so-called Chilean economic miracle by writing, "There are two pieces of bread. You eat two. I eat none. Average consumption: one piece of bread per person." In a very different way, but no less questioning of traditional poetic forms, Soto Román takes the events, protagonists, and discourses from the dictatorship—both the ubiquitous and concealed—to explore their impact in shaping modern-day Chile.

Assembled primarily from found material such as declassified documents, testimonies, interviews, and media files, *11* immerses readers in the state-sponsored terror of Pinochet's dictatorship (1973–1990), with its political persecutions, torture, and disappearances, as well as the dilemmas of documenting human rights violations. *11*'s poetry adopts the form of collage, erasure, and appropriation, the language emerging from censorship and suffocation as experienced under military rule. Soto Román makes no attempt to fill in the blanks, rather he indicates where they are and exercises his own right to censor. By withholding information, mimicking strategies of control employed by the military regime and civilian collaborators, he creates new images and ways of understanding how collective memory of political violence is often manipulated. *11* asks us to understand the past through what has been covered up, to reflect on the spoken and unspoken pieces that interact to construct memory in a country still experiencing the effects of its traumatic history.

Soto Román is and isn't a witness to these atrocities. Born in 1977, he belongs to a generation that grew up bombarded by the military junta's discourses and iconography, false news reports to cover up secret police operations, and a generalized atmosphere of suspicion. Some of these experiences appear explicitly in *11*, such as the drumroll in Radio Cooperativa's newscasts or the monumental plaque mounted in Santiago's Diego Portales building and reproduced in thousands of households via Pinochet's televised speeches, juxtaposing Chile's independence with the date of the coup: "1810 CHILE 1973." These are the sounds and silences, the images and blank spaces in the author's personal memory that recreate the sensation of an era. This emotional memory in *11* is also addressed in the various images, such as a coin put into circulation during this period, helicopter diagrams, a prisoner's escape map, and lists of unidentified bodies.

X X X

11's use of multiple voices and records poses a problem of authorship in the original Spanish version that we saw fit to address through a collaborative translation effort, taken on by eight translators from diverse cultural and professional backgrounds: Alexis Almeida, Daniel Beauregard, Daniel Borzutzky, Whitney DeVos, Patrick Greaney, Robin Myers, Jèssica Pujol Duran, and myself. Numerous questions came up while bringing this book into English. Can the sensation of dictatorship be communicated to readers who may not have experience with a similar past? Would this translation dilute the text's political potential, considering all the specific, situated references? How does censorship translate into another language when translated works necessarily lose parts of their context?

These questions reflect the ethical and aesthetic complexities of translating documentary poetics. In general, we have attempted to preserve the text's testimonial style without overexplaining what may be unknown to an English-speaking audience, in order to convey a sense of confusion or discomfort, very much present in the original. Our translation of *11* is thus an invitation to embrace the uncomfortable and unknowable, to step toward foreign experience as a means of empathy, ultimately to comprehend one's own place in the world.

It is interesting to note that in a project involving so many translators the lines of translation authorship necessarily get blurred. Though we divided the book into different sections for each translator to work on individually, once all the pieces were complete, everyone was given a chance to read through the entire manuscript. This dynamic turned into an intense series of revisions that involved double-checking primary and secondary sources, constructive commentary, and finding creative solutions in a collaborative effort.

If, as Gayatri Spivak says, translation is the most intimate form of reading, translation in this case also became an intimate form of editing, slowly sculpting a text able to stand on its own in English. All of us strongly support bilingual editions, but we believe this translation gains new life in English without having to provide a copy of the original, which would have interfered with the book's textual arrangement and use of blank space. This, of course, obliges readers to trust our version of the book, though it is important to stress that Soto Román, who also happens to be a translator from English to Spanish, actively participated in the review process and certain translation decisions.

As the Anglophone world is becoming increasingly aware of the translator's role in bringing foreign-language literature to readers of English, translators have also increasingly sought new ways to practice our craft, including collaborative projects and translation collectives. Two initiatives on my radar are directly related to *11*: the Colectivo Frank Ocean, in Chile—in which Soto Román participates—has created street posters and memes of their translations of African American, women, and LGBTQI+ authors into Chilean Spanish, intervening in public and virtual spaces; and the North American Free Translation Agreement/No America Fraught Translation Argument (NAFTA), co-founded by Whitney DeVos, which is a group of poet-translators resignifying the literary spaces that traverse the Mexico-U.S.-

Canada borders. Both initiatives connect translation to politics, exploring the relationship between ethics and aesthetics. Without reinforcing the translator's historic invisibility, they introduce new ways of imagining the translator as a collective writer. Reading literature in translation allows us to understand how the idea of a single author is an illusion.

x x x

In October of 2019, mass protests over inequality swept through Chile to initiate a political and social crisis that the country has yet to resolve. Those first months of protest, during Sebastián Piñera's right-wing administration, were met with violent repression reminiscent of the dictatorship: soldiers patrolling the streets, curfews, arbitrary arrests, torture and sexual abuse of detainees, over two dozen protestors killed, and hundreds of people blinded by police pellet gunfire. Four human rights reports documented thousands of cases, but only a handful of police and soldiers have been held accountable. "Never again," the opening phrase of *11* which was used as a slogan to defend human rights after the return to democracy in various South American countries, seemed to lose its meaning in the midst of those turbulent months.

The protests did, however, lead to the creation of a constitutional convention tasked with drafting a new constitution that would replace the presiding Pinochet-era carta magna. The constitution of 1980 introduced an overarching legal structure for free-market policies, often seen as a major obstacle to remedying Chile's profound inequalities. Parts of the actual text, approved in a rigged national referendum, are reproduced in *11*, as is the ballot for that referendum. By mid-2022, millions of Chileans were reading the draft of a new constitution, imagining a more just country that would include amplified fundamental rights, universal healthcare, gender parity in public offices, Indigenous representation in the political sphere, mechanisms to fight corruption, and other structural transformations. While the text topped Chile's bestseller lists for several weeks, voters on

September 4, 2022, rejected the proposal in a mandatory referendum. Misinformation, fear, and the ruling classes once again prevailed. Pinochet's legacy remained intact.

The process of bringing *11* into English has run parallel to the events launched by the 2019 protests. Translating, editing, rereading, and recreating this book in English while Chile was experiencing major historical developments allowed us to see with more clarity the uprooted dreams, violent repression, extended trauma, greed, and powers that have made Chile the country it is today. As translators, we have attempted to tap into what we have witnessed in the past three years in order to reimagine experiences that, while embedded in the memory of one South American country, may offer insight into or new ways of understanding other experiences of political violence throughout the region and elsewhere.

Thomas Rothe
Santiago, October 2022

The poems included in this work were composed using audio and visual material found in documentaries, interviews, articles, and other documents of miscellaneous nature.

Sources consulted include, among others: Political Constitution of the Republic of Chile; The Rettig Report; The Valech Report; The KUBARK Manual; newspaper and magazine archives; "The Cases of the Cardinal Archives" project website, managed by the School of Journalism of the Universidad Diego Portales and Chile's Investigative Journalism Center (CIPER); the Digital Archive of the Miguel Enríquez Study Center; and the archives of the Digital Library of the Museum of Memory and Human Rights.

ACKNOWLEDGMENTS

The original Spanish version of this book was completed thanks to a residence at the MacDowell Colony (Peterborough, New Hampshire), in January 2013.

Various versions of some of the poems in this book have appeared, in Spanish or English, in *The American Poetry Review*, *A Perfect Vacuum*, *Crux Desperationis*, *MAKE Magazine*, *O'clock*, *Periodicities: A Journal of Poetry and Poetics*, *Revista Mandorla*, and *World Literature Today*. Thank you to the editors of these publications for the generosity and interest.

Carlos Soto Román (Valparaíso, 1977) is a poet, translator, and pharmacist. He is the author of *La Marcha de los Quiltros* (1999), *Haikú Minero* (2007), and *Cambio y Fuera* (2009), and the translator into Spanish of *Holocaust* by Charles Reznikoff.

Thomas Rothe's translations include Rodrigo Lira's *Testimony of Circumstances*, and Emma Villazón's *Expendables*. With Lucía Stecher, he has translated Edwidge Danticat's *Create Dangerously* and *Claire of the Sea Light* into Spanish.

Alexis Almeida is a poet and translator. Her translations include Roberta Iannamico's *Wreckage*, Marina Yuszczuk's *Single Mother*, Dalia Rosetti's *Dreams and Nightmares*, and Florencia Castellano's *Monitored Properties*.

Daniel Beauregard is a poet, publisher, and translator. He is the author of the chapbooks *HELLO MY MEAT* and *Before You Were Born*, and a co-founder of OOMPH!, a small press devoted to the publication of poetry and prose in translation.

Daniel Borzutzky is the author of *The Book of Interfering Bodies*, *In the Murmurs of the Rotten Carcass Economy*, *The Performance of Becoming Human*, and *Lake Michigan*. He has translated books by Galo Ghigliotto, Jaime Luis Huenún, and Raúl Zurita.

Whitney DeVos is a writer and translator living in Mexico City, where she is completing a doctoral dissertation on documentary and investigative poetics in the Americas. Her translations have appeared in the *Acentos Review* and the *Chicago Review*.

Patrick Greaney is the co-editor and translator of *An Austrian Avant-Garde* and the author of *Untimely Beggar: Poverty and Power from Baudelaire to Benjamin* and *Quotational Practices: Repeating the Future in Contemporary Art*.

Robin Myers is a Mexico City-based poet and translator. Her translations include *Lyric Poetry Is Dead* by Ezequiel Zaidenwerg, *Animals at the End of the World* by Gloria Susana Esquivel, and *Cars on Fire* by Mónica Ramón Ríos.

Jèssica Pujol Duran is a poet, translator, and researcher. Her books include *Now Worry*, *Every Bit of Light*, *El país pintat*, and *Entrar es tan difícil salir/Enter Exit Is So Difficult*, a bilingual edition with William Rowe. She is the editor of the magazine Alba Londres.